International Finance Perspectives

International Finance Perspectives

Jeff Madura
Florida Atlantic University

Kolb Publishing Company
4705 S.W. 72 Ave.   Miami, Florida 33155
(305) 663-0550   FAX (305) 663-6579

About the Author

Jeff Madura is the Sun Bank Professor of Finance at Florida Atlantic University. He is the author of *International Financial Management* and a co-author of *International Financial Markets*. His research on international financial management has been published in numerous journals, including *Journal of Financial and Quantitative Analysis, Journal of Banking and Finance, Journal of Money, Credit, and Banking, Journal of International Money and Finance, Journal of Financial Research, Global Finance Journal, Journal of Multinational Financial Management, Journal of International Financial Markets, Institutions, and Money, Journal of Portfolio Management, Journal of Financial Services Research,* and *Columbia Journal of World Business.* He has also served as an international consultant for multinational corporations.

Library of Congress Catalog Card Number 92-75277

ISBN: 1-878975-22-6

Kolb Publishing Company
4705 S.W. 72 Ave. Miami, Florida 33155
(305) 663-0550   FAX (305) 663-6579

Preface

Given the increasing globalization of business, students need a thorough understanding of how financial management is modified when applied to international business. Many financial management textbooks contain boxed inserts on international financial management, but the coverage tends to be somewhat limited because of the attention that must be given to all other aspects of financial management. Since *International Finance Perspectives* focuses exclusively on global applications, it can thoroughly "internationalize" courses on financial management.

Intended Market

International Finance Perspectives can serve as a supplement to the introductory, intermediate, or MBA level courses (including case courses) in financial management. Each of the topics covered in this text can be applied to a particular chapter of financial management textbooks. The main theme of the text is how corporate financial policies are affected by global conditions.

Organization of the Text

The organization of topics is structured to match the organization of many textbooks on financial management. One or more topics is provided for each of the typical chapters contained in a financial management text. However, since some of these textbooks follow a different organization (such as covering short-term concepts before long-term concepts), the topics in this text can be rearranged accordingly. The topics are listed in the Table of Contents, along with the typical chapter title of a financial management text to which the topic is related. Each of the topics is self-contained, so that the order of topics can be rearranged to match the corresponding organization in the financial management course.

Acknowledgements

This text benefitted from the suggestions of Robert Kolb (the publisher), and Ricardo Rodriguez (University of Miami). I thank my colleagues, especially Dan McCarty, Ken Wiant, and Emilio Zarruk, for their suggestions. I also wish to thank Carol Annunziato, Rita Crowell, and Joan Hedges for their assistance. I also thank the production staff at Kolb

Publishing: Kateri Davis (production manager), Ginny Guerrant (editor), Diane Rubler (editor), Evelyn Gosnell (graphic artist), and Joe Rodriguez (cover design). Finally, I wish to thank my wife, Mary, and my parents, Arthur and Irene Madura, for their continued moral support.

Contents

4 Impact of Foreign Conditions on Local Interest Rates   26

5 International Financial Markets   32

6 Risk and Return Tradeoffs in International Business   41

16 Multinational Cash Budgeting 108

17 Multinational Cash Management 116

18 Credit Policies of Multinational Corporations 123

19 Inventory Management of Multinational Corporations   129

20 Multinational Short—Term Financing   136

21 Estimating Cash Flows for Possible Foreign Projects   142

22 Multinational Capital Budgeting 148

23 Global Cost of Capital 158

24 Global Capital Structure Policy 165

28 Currency Options   192

29 Integrated Multinational Financial Management   200

Answers to End–of–Chapter Discussion Questions   204

1

Importance of Global Financial Management

Financial management involves a set of tasks undertaken to make investment and financing decisions. The managers assigned to perform these tasks strive to make decisions that maximize the value of the firm. In recent years, numerous business opportunities have become available in response to events such as the unification of European countries, the movement toward free enterprise in Eastern Europe, and the removal of trade barriers in the United States, Canada, and Mexico. Given the new international business opportunities, financial managers can benefit from an understanding of the international environment. Such benefits are obvious for large multinational corporations (MNCs) such as American Brands, Coca Cola, Digital Equipment Corporation, and Ford Motor Company that generate billions of dollars in sales from foreign business every year. However, an understanding of the international environment is also beneficial to smaller firms that consider exporting or importing materials. It is even beneficial to firms that have no international business, but compete with firms that do.

Opportunities Resulting From the Removal of Barriers in Mexico

The removal of some trade barriers between the United States and Mexico can allow some American firms more opportunities to export goods to Mexico. It may also allow some American firms to more easily establish so-called maquiladora factories across the U.S. border, where Mexican labor can be hired for about 90 percent less on average than what is paid for labor on similar work at home.

However, some U.S. firms are now more exposed to the competition from Mexican exporting firms, or from other U.S. firms that have lowered their prices after establishing maquiladoras to produce goods at a lower cost. Even purely domestic firms can be affected by the removal of these trade barriers, because the foreign competition will increase in particular labor-intensive industries.

Opportunities Resulting From the Removal of Barriers in Europe

Many U.S. firms with subsidiaries in Europe perceive major opportunities from the conversion of East European countries to market-based economies. However, with these additional opportunities, there are additional risks. The lower cost of labor in these countries could allow firms established in these countries to penetrate Western European markets through exporting. While some firms could gain market share in this way, other firms will lose market share.

The relaxation of barriers across product markets throughout Europe forces firms to become more efficient. In some cases, firms located in high-wage countries may be unable to compete with those located in low-wage countries, regardless of how efficient they are. Consequently, some firms will need to restructure their operations to capitalize on any comparative advantage that they have over competitors from other countries. This evolutionary process in Europe requires an assessment of the costs and benefits of restructuring possibilities, even for the U.S. firms that do business in Europe. An understanding of financial management and some background in international business is needed to conduct such an assessment. The success or even survival of firms is dependent on these managerial attributes.

How Global Awareness Affects Managerial Decisions

Financial managers are commonly required to make investment decisions. These decisions will dictate the manner by which firms expand over time. Financial managers must determine the potential benefits of various investment alternatives to make proper investment decisions. The measurement of the potential benefits can be enhanced by accounting for international conditions. For example, when Ford Motor Company considers establishing a new subsidiary to build automobiles, it must estimate (1) the demand for automobiles in that country, (2) the tax effects of earnings in that country, (3) costs of financing the foreign subsidiary, and (4) possible exchange movements when future earnings at the subsidiary are remitted to the U.S. When firms such as DuPont, 3M, and Dow consider exporting to a foreign country, they must be able to assess the potential demand for the product in the country, and the impact of possible exchange rate movements on the demand. When Anheuser-Busch considers producing a new premium beer for sale in the U.S., it must consider how the weakening of the German mark can cause the price of German beer sold in the U.S. to decline, which indirectly affects U.S. consumer's demand for its new beer.

The manner by which the expansion of MNCs is dependent on foreign conditions is shown in Figure 1.1. Financial managers of MNCs consider any opportunities that can enhance their cash flows and maximize the stock price. While some opportunities for U.S.-based MNCs are in the U.S., more opportunities tend to be in foreign countries where barriers to international business are being removed.

Integration Between Financial Management and Other Disciplines

Global financial management requires more than expertise in the technical aspects of finance. It also requires an understanding of different tax rules,

Figure 1.1
Impact of Foreign Conditions on the Stock Price of a Multinational Corporation

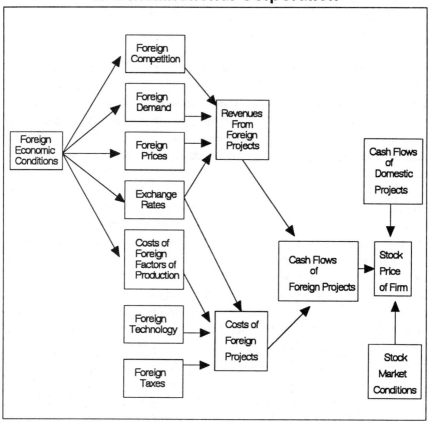

political ideologies, and customs across countries. A successful business in the U.S. would not necessarily be successful in some foreign countries because of these differences. While most financial managers are unable to have expertise in all relevant characteristics that vary across countries, they must at least recognize which characteristics will vary. Other departments within the firm (such as accounting and marketing) may be able to furnish the information necessary for financial managers to make decisions on a global basis. As an example, consider a U.S.-based MNC that assesses the feasibility of establishing a subsidiary in a foreign country. The financial managers must determine whether the project will be feasible. The feasibility of the project is dependent on the following factors, among others:

Factor	Input Needed From
Foreign demand for the product	Marketing Department
Price of the product	Marketing Department and Finance Department
Cost of producing the product	Production Department and Accounting Department
Taxes imposed by host country	Accounting or Tax Department
Host government environmental restrictions	Production Department
Required return on project	Accounting Department and Finance Department

The cost of producing the product in a foreign country can differ substantially from the cost in the U.S. because of differences in wage rates, costs of leasing space, productivity, and costs of financing. Since the price is partially based on cost, the price can vary from what would be charged in the U.S. The foreign demand for the product will be based on the foreign consumer behavior, and the competition for selling the product in that country. The taxes to be imposed are dependent on the tax guidelines of the host country, and the amount of income to be earned by the subsidiary. This example illustrates how a decent feasibility analysis requires input on various characteristics of the foreign country.

Enhancing Global Business Skills

Financial managers in Western Europe tend to have a good understanding of international business because they are accustomed to doing business in other countries. In fact, exports represent 20 percent or more of the gross national product in some European countries. Financial managers in the U.S. tend to have less international business background. However, steps are being taken in the U.S. to enhance global skills. Many American universities have begun to offer more international business courses. In addition, some corporations are implementing programs to help their financial managers and other managers understand international business. For example, some MNCs such as Colgate-Palmolive Co., General Electric, Proctor & Gamble Co., and Pepsi Co., Inc. allow some of their managers to gain international experience by working overseas.

Many smaller companies are less able to enhance their manager's global skills in this way, since they may not even have foreign subsidiaries. Nevertheless, the managers of any companies involved in exporting must have an understanding of foreign customs, foreign economic conditions, and exchange rate movements, since these factors affect demand for exports. Managers of firms involved in exporting and importing need to understand trade financing techniques such as letters of credit.

One way in which U.S. firms are attempting to obtain a more global perspective is by hiring executives from foreign countries who have much experience in global business. For example, in 1992 General Motors hired an executive from Spain to direct its global purchasing, while Xerox hired an executive vice-president from Italy. Executives from large non-U.S. companies not only have experience in global business operations, but also may understand the customs, cultures, and government regulations of several foreign countries.

Managers of all firms must recognize how exchange rate movements can affect their costs and their competitive position. While companies value such managerial skills, they may prefer to hire people that already have the skills rather than train them. Even if the primary job description is not classified as international, an understanding of the global environment is desirable.

How Students Can Obtain Global Business Skills

Given the general trend towards a global marketplace, students should attempt to develop a background that prepares them for global business. While there is no perfect format, some of the ways in which students can gain a "global edge" are as follows:

(1) Take as many international business courses as possible. Even if you wish to focus on a more specialized discipline such as finance, accounting, etc., international business and international marketing courses provide a valuable background for learning about customs, cultures, and consumer behavior across countries. A course on international economics is also valuable because it can explain how exchange rates are affected by economic conditions, and how one country's economy can be influenced by economic conditions in other countries. Students interested in financial management should definitely take a course on international financial management to understand how financial decisions can be affected by a firm's foreign operations or foreign economic conditions.

(2) Consider a foreign–study program for a semester or year. This type of program can educate you from a foreign perspective. Students and professors will likely come from diverse cultures. In addition, your experience in a foreign country will help you understand firsthand how customs, cultures, and business conditions differ from the U.S.

(3) Learn a foreign language. Students with the ability to speak and write in a foreign language are considered more seriously for positions at foreign subsidiaries.

(4) Develop an interest in global topics. Many business courses now attempt to include some global applications. Pay special attention to these applications. If your course requires a term paper, consider a global business topic. Popular business magazines such as *Business Week*, *Forbes*, and *Fortune* cover many global issues. Pay attention to these issues.

Summary

The progress toward removal of cross-border barriers should result in global markets. Financial managers must have global business skills so that they can capitalize on international opportunities, or can defend against foreign competition. Students who enhance their global business skills are not only more prepared to work in a global marketplace, but also enhance their marketability and mobility in the job market.

Discussion

Some of the more typical financial decisions of a corporation include whether to invest in specific projects, how to finance the projects, where to obtain funds, how to invest excess cash, and how much to pay shareholders in the form of dividends. The financial decisions for an MNC are often more complex. Review Figure 1.2 for Jordan Company, a U.S.-based MNC with three foreign subsidiaries. Jordan conducts international business through its foreign subsidiaries. In addition, the U.S. parent exports its products (medical supplies) to the United Kingdom and imports some materials from Mexico. The parent developed the subsidiaries several years ago, and receives remitted earnings from the subsidiaries on an annual basis. The "Discussion" section of each global application in this text applies the concepts to Jordan Co.

(a) Describe some of the more obvious types of financial decisions by Jordan Co. that relate to its international business.

(b) How might Jordan Co. attempt to benefit from the reduction in barriers in Mexico and in Eastern Europe?

Figure 1.2
Illustration of Jordan's International Business

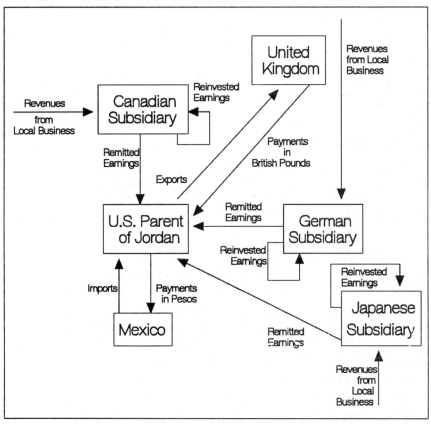

2

Agency Problems Resulting From Global Business

A firm's financial managers are expected to serve in the best interests of the shareholders. That is, their objective should be to serve as agents for shareholders in which they maximize shareholder wealth. Yet, financial managers may be tempted to make decisions that serve their own interests rather than the shareholders'. The potential conflict between the goals of managers and shareholders causes agency problems. To assure that managers make decisions that serve the interests of shareholders, agency costs are incurred. Those firms that are involved with global business have unique characteristics that affect potential agency problems, as discussed below.

Agency Problems of Foreign Subsidiaries

To illustrate the potential agency costs of a U.S.-based multinational corporation (MNC), consider that many MNCs have subsidiaries in various countries that produce and/or sell products in those countries. The use of subsidiaries may be more efficient than producing the goods in the U.S. and exporting them to the foreign countries. The subsidiaries tend to periodically remit portions of their profits to the U.S. parent (headquarters).

Assume that each subsidiary's performance is dependent on the profits it generates. Under these conditions, managers of each subsidiary are likely to make decisions that are based on local conditions, while ignoring the impact of these decisions on the overall value of the firm.

For example, a subsidiary in a developing country may decide to expand the business there because the perceived benefits to the subsidiary exceed the costs. Assume the expansion is financially supported by the parent. Revenues received by the subsidiary may appear to be large if the host country's government imposes low taxes on the revenues. However, the earnings remitted to the U.S. parent may be taxed by the U.S. government. (This depends on the amount of tax paid to the host country, among other factors). In addition, if the currency of the host country depreciates (declines) against the dollar over time, any revenues sent to the U.S. parent will convert to fewer dollars. The revenues may appear to be high from the subsidiary's perspective, but be low when the currency is converted into U.S. dollars. Thus, the project could reduce the value of the overall MNC even though it was beneficial to the subsidiary.

This example illustrates an agency problem because a decision is made without considering the impact on the entire MNC. This type of agency problem is especially common when subsidiary managers make decisions that are intended solely to enhance the value of the subsidiary.

As a second example, consider a case in which one subsidiary of the MNC is adversely affected by a general weakness in the Japanese yen, while another subsidiary of the MNC is adversely affected by a strong yen but benefits from a weaker yen. Since the effects of a changing yen value on the subsidiaries are somewhat offsetting, the impact on the MNC overall may be negligible. Yet, if each subsidiary is focused on how its performance will be affected, it may attempt to hedge against the impact. If there are offsetting effects, the subsidiaries should not attempt to hedge against the risk, since hedging strategies require time and transactions costs. The costs to subsidiaries are higher when they focus on their own performance rather than the overall performance of the MNC.

Influence of Country Characteristics on Agency Problems

Even if the parent attempts to assure that the subsidiary's managers serve the best interests of the MNC, other characteristics of MNCs heighten the agency problem, as discussed below.

Diversity of Operations Across Foreign Subsidiaries

For MNCs that have diverse operations across subsidiaries, it may be more difficult for the parent to monitor the subsidiaries. Each foreign subsidiary would have to be monitored without comparison to the other subsidiaries, because differences in procedures and performance could be attributed to the diversity in operations. Conversely, if all foreign subsidiaries had similar operations, some procedures could be standardized across subsidiaries. Thus, the parent would be able to more easily detect any deviation from the norm by a particular subsidiary.

Distance Between Parent and Each Subsidiary

The distance between the parent and each subsidiary can make it difficult for the parent to monitor them. Since executives of the parent are unable to travel to distant subsidiaries frequently, these subsidiaries are subject to less monitoring and are more likely to make decisions that conflict with the goal of maximizing shareholder wealth.

Appeal of Subsidiary Locations

The monitoring by parent's executives may be focused only on the subsidiaries in more desirable locations, which could cause excessive travel expenses, another agency problem. If a U.S.-based MNC had one subsidiary in Australia and a second subsidiary in a cold, less developed country, the U.S. parent's executives may be tempted to visit the Australian subsidiary frequently, but to avoid the other subsidiary. Consequently, travel costs to Australia may waste corporate funds. In addition, agency problems may develop at the other subsidiary since it is not being monitored by the U.S. parent.

Accounting Rules of Host Countries

Another characteristic of global business that can cause agency problems is the disparity in accounting rules across countries. It is difficult for the parent of an MNC to compare financial statement items across subsidiaries of different countries to measure performance. Thus, a foreign subsidiary may be able to overstate its performance, which causes monitoring problems for the parent.

Customs of Host Countries

Different languages and customs can make it more difficult for the parent to monitor subsidiary managers. For example, the custom in some countries is for the firm to be somewhat lenient on the credit policy if a client firm is experiencing financial problems. Bribes are considered to be acceptable in some countries, and may cause managers of the foreign subsidiaries to make decisions based on their personal gains. Thus, the subsidiary's management may deviate from the objectives of the parent without necessarily attempting to serve their own best interests.

A related agency problem experienced by MNCs is that their subsidiaries may offer expensive special programs for enhancing social conditions when doing business in their countries. The subsidiaries may engage in some programs that will not necessarily serve the best interests of the MNC's shareholders. This is especially likely in countries where there is some tradition for firms to offer such programs. Managers who were raised in these countries may tend to follow tradition, possibly at the expense of the MNC's shareholders (unless the programs somehow generate cash flows for the MNC).

Performance Measurement and Agency Problems of Subsidiaries

Agency costs can arise when a parent has difficulty monitoring the operations and performance of its subsidiaries. To illustrate such monitoring problems, consider a U.S.-based MNC with five subsidiaries that perform the same operations, but are located in five different countries. Would it be fair to monitor each subsidiary by comparing its costs and revenues to those of other subsidiaries? Not necessarily! One subsidiary's costs of producing a product may be higher than the others simply because it is located in a high-wage country, not because it is inefficient. Revenues generated by one subsidiary country may be lower in a given year because prices charged in that country are lower, not because the number of units sold was lower. Even when measured by units sold, one subsidiary may perform worse than the others because of a relatively poor economy in that host country, which can not be controlled by the subsidiary.

Furthermore, the comparison of profitability among subsidiaries can be distorted by exchange rates. How does a Canadian subsidiary's earnings of 40 million Canadian dollars in a given year compare to a British subsidiary's earnings of 20 million British pounds? The earnings figures could be translated to a common denominator such as the U.S. dollar, but the outcome is then biased by the prevailing exchange rate at that time. For example, if the pound is relatively strong at the time of the translation while the Canadian dollar is weak, the British subsidiary's earnings will probably translate to a larger U.S. dollar figure. Conversely, if the Canadian dollar is strong while the pound is weak, the Canadian subsidiary's earnings will appear to be higher. A related issue is how to measure performance? Should the parent use a subsidiary's earnings before taxes as a benchmark, or earnings after taxes? How should the earnings of each parent be adjusted for the size of the parent? If each subsidiary produced a different product, the comparison among foreign subsidiaries would be even more difficult, because there are differences in industry competition for each product, which could affect the subsidiary's performance.

Given these types of monitoring problems, managers of subsidiaries may believe that the parent can not properly measure the contribution of the subsidiary to the wealth of the shareholders who own the MNC. Thus, the managers are encouraged to make decisions that are in the interests of themselves rather than those of the shareholders. The more pronounced the problems are involved in monitoring the contribution of a subsidiary to shareholder wealth, the more tempted managers are to deviate from this goal, and the agency costs are higher.

How to Reduce Agency Problems at Foreign Subsidiaries

While there is no perfect solution for MNCs to minimize agency costs, some general rules can be considered. First, the goals should be clearly communicated to the subsidiaries, so that subsidiary managers consider the effects of any policy decisions on the MNC overall. This can be accomplished by frequent communication between the parent and the managers of foreign subsidiaries. Each subsidiary should state its operational plans on a periodic basis. If the parent approves of the plans, it can monitor performance by determining whether the subsidiary met its goals each quarter or so. To the extent that performance can be measured from financial statements, executives of the parent would not need to visit the subsidiaries frequently.

The parent and each subsidiary may set goals on the total production to be achieved by that subsidiary, production costs, and the total sales level. While the production characteristics are not directly affected by the economy, the total sales level is. Nevertheless, a target sales level could be established and then adjusted if economic conditions change significantly. Because of differences in economic conditions across the host countries of the subsidiaries and the differences in the business operations across subsidiaries, the parent may monitor each subsidiary in relation to that subsidiary's previous performance (after adjusting for changes in economic conditions of that country).

Figure 2.1 illustrates the possible interactions between foreign subsidiaries and the U.S. parent for one product line produced by the MNC. The long-term goals are determined by the parent, with the input of subsidiaries. Managers at subsidiaries make the day-to-day decisions to keep their subsidiaries operating. Any major decisions such as expansion are assessed by the regional vice-president of that product line and/or by the parent's vice-president of that product line, who may oversee all worldwide operations for that product. While this figure gives the appearance of a centralized organization, most decisions may be made by the individual subsidiaries. The regional or parent vice-president may be responsible for assuring that the subsidiary motives are consistent with long-term goals established for the entire MNC.

To deal with the different accounting systems across countries, the MNC's parent could request a standardized financial statement for all

Figure 2.1
Interaction Between Multinational Managers

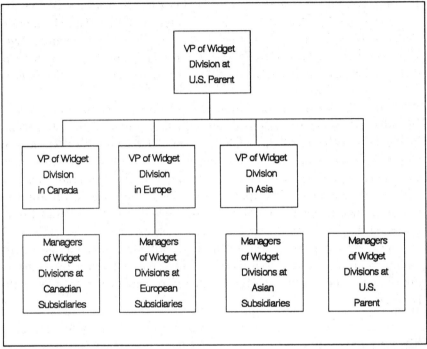

subsidiaries, even if these statements could not be used to satisfy each country's reporting requirements. In this way, the parent may be more able to monitor the performance of each subsidiary. Separate financial statements could be completed to accommodate host government reporting requirements. When confronted with other host government requirements such as social programs, the subsidiaries should consider implementing whatever programs can enhance their image and visibility, so that there may be some payback to the subsidiaries.

Summary

In summary, financial managers of foreign subsidiaries may be tempted to make decisions that serve their own interests rather than shareholder interests, because they may not be closely monitored by the parent. Even if a parent attempts to closely monitor foreign subsidiaries, it may be difficult because of country characteristics that can distort the relative performance of subsidiaries.

Some degree of centralization is needed to assure that the goals of subsidiaries are clearly specified in a way that is consistent with serving in the best interests of the MNC's shareholders. Given differences in economic conditions and accounting standards across countries, each subsidiary should be assigned a set of unique goals. The goals could be adjusted if economic conditions change. This form of goal setting does not mean that the decision making is centralized. The subsidiaries can be managed by their respective managers, once the goals have been approved by the parent. The goals are specified so that the subsidiary managers are encouraged to follow guidelines that will ultimately enhance the overall value of the MNC, and therefore benefit the MNC's shareholders.

Discussion

The parent of Jordan Co. is presently assessing the performance of its foreign subsidiaries in Toronto, Canada and Tokyo, Japan.

(a) Explain why the agency costs of Jordan's Japanese subsidiary may be higher than the agency costs of the Canadian subsidiary.

(b) Assume the Japanese yen depreciated against the U.S. dollar, while the Canadian dollar appreciated against the U.S. dollar over the last year. If earnings in each subsidiary are translated into dollars for comparative performance purposes, which of the two subsidiaries would likely show higher performance? How could this type of impact cause agency problems if it was not accounted for?

(c) The Japanese subsidiary requested financial support from the parent of Jordan Company to undertake a major expansion throughout the country. It justified its request by showing evidence that the earnings to the subsidiary would likely increase substantially as a result of the expansion. Assuming that the subsidiary is correct, why might this expansion conflict with the goal of maximizing the wealth of Jordan's shareholders?

3

Global Taxes and Cash Flow

Most financial decisions by firms are based on expected cash flows. Once firms have forecasted future cash flows, they can determine excess cash or deficient cash in various periods. This enables them to assess available funds that can be invested in other projects, or how much additional funds must be borrowed to support existing projects. Cash flows must also be estimated for proposed projects to determine whether these projects should be implemented. Taxes must be estimated when forecasting future cash flows because cash is needed to make tax payments. Since tax rates vary among countries, the cash flows may depend on the country where the business operations occur. Thus, the financing and investment decisions may also be affected.

Global Tax Differentials

Consider a U.S.-based multinational corporation (MNC) with subsidiaries in Europe. The corporate income taxes in Europe will typically be higher than corporate taxes in the U.S. Since a subsidiary's earnings are subject to the foreign tax laws, each subsidiary's cash flows will be affected by its respective host country's tax rules.

MNCs frequently attempt to estimate the cash flows that their subsidiaries will remit to the headquarters (the "parent") over time. This task requires the consideration of withholding taxes imposed by the host country on funds remitted by the subsidiaries to the parent. For example, a host country may require a 10 percent tax on any earnings remitted by the foreign subsidiary to the parent. Numerous countries, including the U.S., impose withholding taxes on earnings sent by a local subsidiary to the parent. The cash flows received by the parent will be reduced whenever withholding taxes are to be paid.

The corporate income and withholding taxes charged by host countries can discourage international business. Figure 3.1 illustrates the possible tax drains from the point at which earnings are generated by international business to the time shareholders receive dividends as a result of this business. These earnings can be reduced because of corporate income taxes paid to the host country, withholding taxes paid to the host country, and corporate income taxes paid to the U.S. government as the earnings are remitted to the U.S. Furthermore, the portion of the residual distributed to shareholders as dividends is subject to taxes.

Tax treaties have been established among countries to prevent double-taxation. These treaties are necessary to encourage global expansion. While these treaties can prevent double-taxation, taxes can still vary across an MNC's subsidiaries according to the country where they are located.

When an MNC's subsidiaries conduct business with each other, they may attempt to price the transactions to account for differences in tax laws. The pricing of these types of transactions is known as transfer pricing. For example, if a subsidiary in a low-tax country purchases supplies from a subsidiary in a high-tax country, a lower price charged for the transactions would reduce the costs and therefore raise the earnings of the low-tax subsidiary. It would also reduce the earnings of the high-tax subsidiary. Even if the consolidated earnings were not affected, the total taxes paid may be reduced as a result of this transfer pricing.

Many countries require that the prices charged by one subsidiary to another be the same as for transactions conducted with unrelated customers. Transfer pricing policies would be more restricted under these circumstances. Nevertheless, there are numerous examples of inter-

Figure 3.1
Illustration of Possible Taxes Paid on
Income from International Business

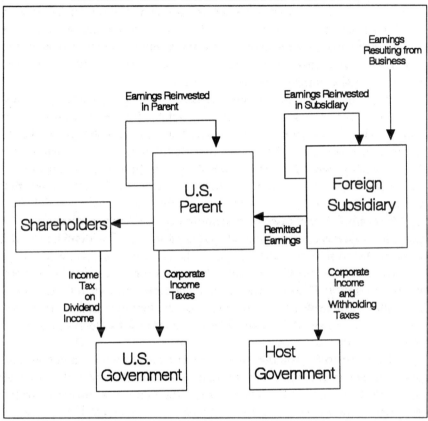

subsidiary transactions in which the profits tend to heavily favor one subsidiary over another.

Estimating Cash Flows of an MNC

The estimation of cash flows is necessary for an MNC to make financial decisions. The cash flows of MNCs are more difficult to estimate than cash flows of domestic firms because of factors unique to the operations of MNCs. These factors are discussed below.

Global Factors Affecting an MNC's Cash Flows

As mentioned earlier, the corporate income tax rates vary across subsidiaries, which can affect the cash flows ultimately received by the parent as a result of international business. Second, withholding taxes may be imposed on funds remitted to the parent. Third, a host government may "block" funds from being remitted by the subsidiary for several years. Some countries such as Columbia, Ecuador, Egypt, Greece, and Mexico typically enforce some restrictions on the proportion of subsidiary earnings that can be remitted to a parent residing outside the country. The cash flows generated by the subsidiary are not affected by these restrictions, but the amount of funds to be remitted to the parent is affected.

A fourth factor that affects parent cash flows is the exchange rate. Consider a German subsidiary of a U.S.-based MNC that was expected to remit DM10 million (DM represents deutsche marks) over each of the next five years to the U.S. parent. These funds are converted to dollars as they are remitted. Since the exchange rate of the mark with respect to the dollar varies over time, there is some uncertainty about the dollar value of the funds to be received by the parent. For example, if a mark was worth $.41, (as it was at the beginning of 1986) the DM10 million would convert to $4,100,000 in a given year. If a mark was worth $.67 (as it was at the beginning of 1991), the DM10 million would convert to $6,700,000. Thus, the cash flows received by the parent will be sensitive to exchange rate movements.

What Cash Flows Are Relevant?

A critical question when analyzing the cash flows of an MNC is what cash flows should be measured? The subsidiary's cash flows only? The parent's cash flows? To answer this question, put yourself in the position of a domestic firm that is considering establishing a foreign subsidiary. Your domestic firm should only invest funds in such a project if the benefits received outweigh the costs. The benefits to the domestic firm from establishing a subsidiary represent the cash flows that are ultimately remitted by the foreign subsidiary. Thus, when assessing the feasibility of a foreign project from the parent's perspective, the relevant cash flows of the foreign project are those associated directly with the parent.

To illustrate this point, consider this extreme example. Assume your firm establishes a small retail store in a less developed country, because there is no competitor in that country for the product you sell. Assume that the host country enforces a restriction that earnings of foreign subsidiaries in its country can not ever be remitted to their respective parents' companies. In this case, the parent's investment in the project will never be recaptured, because it will never directly receive any cash flows from the project. Even if the subsidiary is very profitable, the parent will not reap any benefits. The point of this example is that the relevant cash flows must be assessed from the perspective of whoever is investing the funds in the project. What is good for a foreign subsidiary is not always good for the parent.

Impact of Exchange Rates on Cash Flows of MNCs with Subsidiaries

Since exchange rate movements vary among currencies, future cash flows remitted by each of several subsidiaries would require separate estimates of each respective local currency with respect to the dollar. The currency values of industrialized countries tend to move in the same direction against the dollar (although not by the exact same amount). When these currencies strengthen against the dollar, the cash flows to the parent are enhanced. Conversely, when these currencies weaken, the cash flows to the parent are worth less. This implies that when the currencies are weaker than expected, the cash flows to the parent are less than expected, so that there is a higher probability of a cash deficiency. In fact, if the currencies that have recently weakened are expected to strengthen in the future, the parent may instruct its subsidiaries to refrain from remitting funds. The funds may be reinvested in the host country, rather than converted to dollars at an unfavorable exchange rate. These decisions will also be influenced by the opportunities in the host country. If the subsidiary could either invest in securities (such as Treasury bills) at a relatively high yield in the host country, or could use the funds to support its business operations, it may benefit from retaining the funds until the local currency strengthens against the dollar.

Summary

Cash flows of an MNC are affected by tax differentials across countries and exchange rates. Thus, cash flows to the subsidiary may differ substantially from the cash flows to the parent. Since managers of MNCs frequently estimate cash flows, they must recognize the potential effects of tax differentials and exchange rates. They should also recognize that the effects on cash flows may vary with the perspective (parent versus subsidiary) of concern.

Discussion

Review Figure 3.2 for Jordan Company, a U.S.-based MNC. This diagram shows how the earnings generated by Jordan's subsidiaries are sometimes reinvested to support existing operations, or are remitted to the U.S. parent.

(a) Based on a review of Figure 3.2, explain the various possible ways in which taxes will affect the cash flows that shall ultimately be received by Jordan's parent.

(b) Explain why changes in Germany's tax laws could cause a shift in Jordan's global operations.

Figure 3.2
Cash Flow Diagram for Jordan Co.

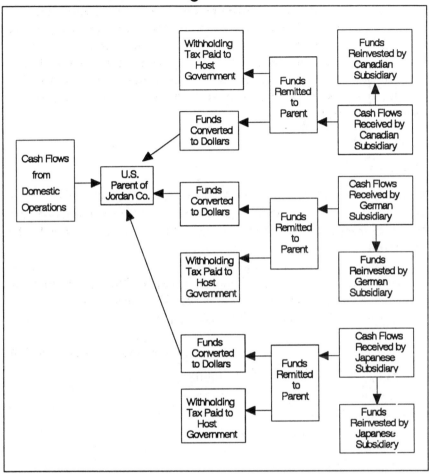

4

Impact of Foreign Conditions on Local Interest Rates

Firms monitor financial market conditions that influence interest rates when making investment and financing decisions. The level of interest rates can affect a firm's decisions, such as whether to expand, whether to issue debt or equity, or whether to borrow short-term versus long-term funds. Since financial markets are globally integrated, local financial market conditions can be influenced by foreign markets. For this reason, firms must monitor foreign financial markets as well, even if their business is completely domestic. Foreign markets can influence a firm's financial policies by affecting the structure of interest rates as explained here.

How Foreign Conditions Affect Interest Rates

The nominal interest rate in any country is made up of a nominal risk-free rate and a risk premium. The nominal risk-free rate is defined here as the yield offered on a security that is free from default risk, such as a Treasury bond. The default risk represents the additional yield required to compensate for the default risk of the firm. Thus, for any corporation issuing a bond, the default risk premium is measured as the difference between the yield of this bond and the yield of a Treasury bond with the same maturity. Figure 4.1 shows how bond yields of various countries tend to move together. This occurs because the demand and supply conditions for funds are globally integrated, as discussed in detail below.

Global Integration of Credit Markets

Nominal risk-free interest rates in any country are affected by the supply and demand for funds in credit markets. Because these markets are somewhat integrated, any changes in the supply and/or demand for funds in one country can transfer to another. As funds flow between countries, the supply and/or demand for funds is altered, thereby affecting the local risk-free interest rate. For example, foreign investors commonly provide more than 30 percent of the funds borrowed by the U.S. Treasury at Treasury auctions. The foreign investment creates a larger supply of funds in the U.S., which places downward pressure on U.S. interest rates. Without the infusion of foreign funds, interest rates paid by the Treasury on borrowed funds would be higher.

Some financial market conditions can place upward pressure on local interest rates. For example, when the Berlin Wall was torn down in 1989, the unification of East and West Germany resulted in an increased demand for loanable funds in Germany. As U.S. investors used funds to accommodate this need, less funds were invested in the U.S. Consequently, this single event caused a reduction in the supply of available funds for the U.S., placing upward pressure on the long-term U.S. interest rates.

Figure 4.1
Government Bond Yields Across Countries

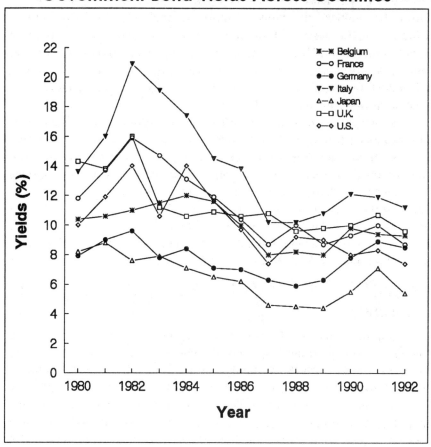

Influence of Foreign Government Policies on U.S. Interest Rates

U.S. rates can also be affected by foreign budget deficits. Rising foreign budget deficits place upward pressure on foreign interest rates, which in turn can attract investment from the U.S. and reduce the supply of available funds in the U.S.

Central banks of foreign countries can indirectly influence the U.S. interest rates by implementing monetary policy. For example, assume that the Bank of England (the central bank of England) uses a monetary policy that reduces the money supply in England. This will cause a reduction in the supply of loanable funds in England, and will place upward pressure on British interest rates. If British interest rates rise and some U.S. investors attempt to capitalize on the high British rates, this will reduce the supply of loanable funds in the U.S. Consequently, U.S. interest rates would rise as well.

Another way in which international conditions can affect U.S. interest rates is through their effect on U.S. inflation. Assume that foreign inflation rises, thereby making foreign imports more expensive. U.S. inflation may increase as a result, since U.S. firms that import supplies may incur higher costs. In addition, U.S. firms that compete with foreign firms for business in the U.S. may increase their prices, as foreign firms are priced out of the market because of high foreign inflation. As U.S. inflation increases, the nominal interest rate in the U.S. typically increases as well to retain the real (inflation-adjusted) interest rate.

Integration of Default Risk Premiums Across Countries

Like nominal risk-free interest rates, default risk premiums can be integrated among countries. Consider that the average default risk premium on funds borrowed by corporations reflects the average premium required by lenders to compensate for default risk. During a weak economy, the probability of default is relatively high and therefore the default risk premium is relatively high. To the extent that economic conditions are related across countries, the perceived levels of default risk across countries should be related as well. Default risk premiums were relatively high in countries during 1982-1983 and 1991-1992 periods when economies were generally weak in most countries.

In summary, each component of the nominal interest rate (risk-free rate and default risk premium) is integrated across countries, which causes nominal interest rates to be integrated as well.

Impact of Increasing Market Integration

Some barriers between countries cause markets to be partially segmented. For example, the lack of information about a foreign country's securities, yields, and tax laws on foreign income earned may discourage investors from investing their funds in foreign countries. Information about such financial characteristics of countries is becoming more accessible, which should increase the transactions between countries. The result of more frequent transactions between countries is greater integration between the nominal interest rates among countries. However, markets will continue to be at least partially segmented because of exchange rate risk. Investors that attempt to capitalize on high interest rates in a foreign country can be adversely affected if the currency denominating the foreign investment depreciates against the investor's home currency over the investment horizon. This implies that the price paid per unit of foreign currency to initiate the foreign investment was more than the price received per unit when the proceeds from the foreign investment were exchanged back to the investor's currencies.

If the foreign currency appreciates, there is a favorable effect on the yield to the investor. However, the uncertainty of the future value of the foreign currency may discourage a flow of funds from one country to another. For this reason, interest rates will not be exactly the same across all countries, even if all other cross-border barriers are eliminated.

How Foreign Conditions Affect the Term Structure

International conditions may even affect the term structure of interest rates. Consider a situation in which an upward sloping yield curve exists in the U.S. Assume a sudden large foreign investment in U.S. bonds, with very little foreign investment in U.S. money market securities. The foreign flow of funds will likely place downward pressure on the yields offered on long-term securities, with no effect on yields of short-term securities. The yield curve should become flatter or downward sloping as a result of the international flow of funds. Since some U.S. firms assess the yield curve when deciding whether to borrow long-term or short-term funds, international financial market conditions indirectly influence the firm's financial decisions by affecting the shape of the yield curve.

Summary

Since foreign conditions tend to influence U.S. interest rates and the U.S. term structure, U.S. firms that forecast U.S. interest rates must monitor foreign conditions. If they can determine how foreign interest rates will change in the future, they may be able to determine how such changes will affect U.S. interest rates. While other economic variables also affect interest rates, firms must account for international financial market conditions in addition to the other variables.

Just as U.S. interest rates are influenced by foreign interest rates, it should be mentioned that the U.S. interest rates can affect foreign interest rates. Thus, U.S.-based MNCs with foreign subsidiaries should consider this type of influence when attempting to forecast interest rates in the foreign countries where they are doing business.

Discussion

Assume that Jordan's medical supplies are often purchased by firms with borrowed funds, so that the demand for supplies is inversely related to interest rate movements (because the demand for supplies is greater when the cost of funds is low). Also assume that a high government budget deficit in Germany is expected to increase the demand for loanable funds there. High inflationary expectations in Canada will affect interest rates there. A shift in Japanese savings from the U.S. banks back to Japanese banks was expected to influence the interest rates there.

(a) Explain how the interest rates in Germany, Canada, Japan, and the U.S. should change.

(b) Explain how Jordan's sales overall will be affected by the events described above.

5

International Financial Markets

Corporations that conduct any global business must not only understand the global product markets where their products are sold, but also the global financial markets. The main global financial markets used by corporations are the foreign exchange markets, the Eurocurrency market, the Eurocredit market, the Eurobond market, and international stock markets. Each of these markets is described below.

Foreign Exchange Markets

Any firm that needs to exchange one currency for another uses the foreign exchange market. The market is composed of numerous commercial banks that serve as intermediaries in this market. These banks maintain inventories of currencies to accommodate the needs of firms and individuals.

Firms can purchase a currency in the spot market (for immediate exchange) or in the forward market (for a specified future date). The forward market is typically used by firms that wish to lock in the exchange rate for a future time. For example, U.S. exporting firms that will receive French francs 90 days from now can engage in a forward contract to exchange the francs for dollars 90 days from now. U.S.

importing firms that will need to pay British pounds in 120 days to pay for imports can engage in a forward contract to exchange dollars for pounds 120 days from now.

The forward exchange rate for a specific future date will not necessarily be equal to the spot exchange rate. Both the spot and forward exchange rates are market determined and therefore respond to various economic conditions.

Factors Affecting Exchange Rate Movements

Since exchange rates are market determined, they change over time in response to changes in the demand for the currency or the supply of the currency for sale in the foreign exchange market. The exchange rates of six major currencies are illustrated in Figure 5.1. From this figure, it is obvious that exchange rates are quite volatile, and therefore can have a major effect on the cash flows resulting from international business. The European currencies tend to move in tandem against the dollar, as is verified in Figure 5.1.

Firms attempt to forecast exchange rates of currencies that they will be purchasing or selling in the future so that they can forecast their future cash flows. They can also use the forecasts to decide whether to engage in forward contracts. Five factors that influence the demand and supply conditions are: (1) inflation differentials, (2) national income differentials, (3) trade barriers, (4) interest rate differentials, and (5) central bank intervention. To illustrate how each of these factors can affect exchange rate movements, we shall focus on the value of the German Mark with respect to the dollar.

Inflation Differentials. Assume that inflation in the U.S. suddenly rises while German inflation remains low. The sudden change in relative prices in the two countries may encourage a stronger U.S. demand for German goods, and a reduced German demand for U.S. goods. Consequently, there is an increased demand for marks (to buy the German goods) and a reduced supply of German marks for sale (by German purchasers of U.S. goods) in the foreign exchange market. Given the reduced supply of marks to be sold to banks in the foreign exchange market along with the increased demand for marks, there is upward pressure on the value of the mark.

International Financial Markets   **33**

Figure 5.1
Exchange Rate Movements Across Currencies

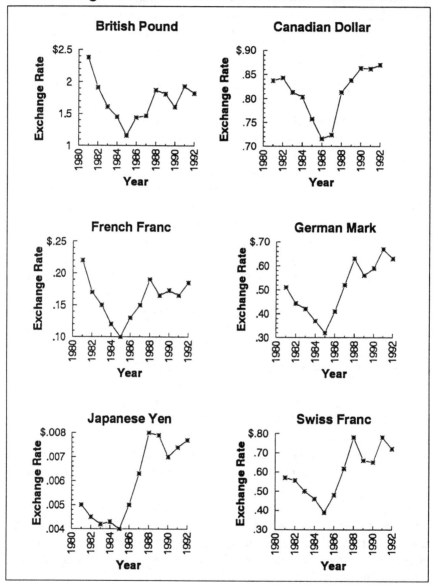

According to the theory of purchasing power parity (PPP), exchange rates adjust by the amount of the differential in inflation between countries. For example, if the inflation in the U.S. is 1 percent, while the inflation in Germany is 4 percent, German consumers will increase their demand for dollars to buy U.S. products (to capitalize on relatively low U.S. prices) and U.S. consumers will reduce their demand for German marks to buy German products (to avoid the increase in German prices). If all other factors were held constant, the mark would have to depreciate by three percentage points to create parity in the purchasing power among products of the two countries. At this point, the U.S. consumers could either buy U.S. products that experienced a 1 percent increase (because of the 1 percent inflation there) or buy German products that are now priced 1 percent higher from their perspective (because of 4 percent German inflation, minus the 3 percent savings from the depreciation of the mark). The German consumers could either buy products that are now priced 4 percent higher (because of the 4 percent inflation there) or buy U.S. products that are now priced 4 percent higher from their perspective (because of 1 percent U.S. inflation plus the 3 percent increase in costs from the depreciation of the mark).

This theory explains why currencies of countries that experience relatively high inflation tend to depreciate over time. However, the actual relationship between inflation differentials and exchange rates is not so precise, because other factors also affect exchange rates.

National Income Differentials.   To consider how national income differentials can affect exchange rates, assume that the German income increases substantially, while the U.S. income remains unchanged. Other things being equal, this should cause an increase in the German demand for U.S. goods. The supply of marks to be exchanged for dollars would increase (implying an increased German demand for dollars), which causes downward pressure on the mark's value. If the national income of the U.S. rose by a larger amount than the German income, the opposite effect would be expected, other things being equal.

Trade Barriers.   To consider how trade barriers can affect exchange rates, assume that the U.S. places a strict quota on goods imported from Germany. In this case, U.S. purchases of German goods would decline, which implies a reduced U.S. demand for marks. If there is no retaliation by the German government, this should place downward pressure on the value of the mark. If trade barriers were imposed on goods sent from the U.S. to Germany, the opposite effect would occur.

Interest Rate Differentials.

To consider how interest rate differentials affect exchange rates, assume that the U.S. interest rate rises while the German interest rate remains unchanged. Since the U.S. interest rates may make the U.S. securities more attractive, there may be an increased German demand for U.S. securities, which reflects an increase in the supply of marks to be exchanged by German investors. There may even be a reduced U.S. demand for German securities, which reflects a reduced demand for marks. Both forces place downward pressure on the value of the mark. If German interest rates rose while U.S. interest rates declined or remained constant, the opposite effects would occur, other things being equal. In fact, the relatively high German interest rates in 1992 were cited as the key reason for the mark's strength at that time.

Central Bank Intervention.

To consider how central bank intervention could influence exchange rates, assume that the Federal Reserve, the central bank of the U.S., exchanged some of its dollar reserves which were previously maintained outside the foreign exchange market, for German marks. Its exchange of dollars for marks reflects additional demand for marks, which places upward pressure on the value of the mark. If the Federal Reserve or some other central bank exchanged German mark reserves (that were previously held outside of the foreign exchange market) for dollars, the opposite effect would occur, other things being equal.

Since exchange rates are affected simultaneously by all factors just discussed, it is difficult to assess how they will move in the future. Firms may attempt to forecast movements by forecasting how the factors will change, and estimating the potential impact the factors have on exchange rates.

Eurocurrency Market

Foreign subsidiaries of U.S. firms commonly use the Eurocurrency market for short-term investing or financing. The Eurocurrency market is composed of numerous commercial banks (called Eurobanks) that accept deposits and provide loans in various foreign currencies. Thus, a subsidiary that has excess cash denominated in one or more foreign currencies may place a deposit with a Eurobank. Meanwhile, other subsidiaries that are short of funds can borrow from the Eurobank. The Eurobank serves as an intermediary by channeling funds from the firms with excess cash to the firms with cash deficiencies. The interest charged by the Eurobank on loans will be slightly higher than the rate it offered on deposits denominated in the same currency.

Eurocredit Market

Foreign subsidiaries of U.S. firms use the Eurocredit market to obtain intermediate loans. Eurobanks serve this market by channeling deposited funds to corporations in the form of Eurocredit loans. The interest rate charged to corporate borrowers is determined as a premium above the existing London Interbank Offer Rate (LIBOR), the rate charged on loans in the currency of concern between Eurobanks. There is a different LIBOR for each currency. The interest rate on Eurocredit loans usually adjusts periodically (such as once a year) to LIBOR. Since LIBOR is market determined, the interest rate on Eurocredit loans moves in accordance with market interest rates.

Eurobond Market

Firms can obtain long-term funds from the Eurobond market, which is a well-established market where bonds denominated in different currencies are placed. A syndicate of investment banks from various countries places the bonds across investors. Firms that engage in international business sometimes denominate bonds in foreign currencies, since they may need these currencies to expand their international operations, and can use proceeds from international operations to repay their debt.

International Stock Markets

Firms can also obtain long-term funds by issuing stock in foreign countries. A syndicate of investment banks can help place the stock in one or more countries. Many of the Eurobanks that serve as intermediaries in the Eurocurrency and Eurocredit markets also act as investment banks to place bonds and stocks for MNCs.

The issuing firm may desire to enhance its global image by issuing stock in one or more foreign markets, and therefore may decide to obtain funds in these markets rather than in its home market. Some firms may believe that they can more easily sell their stock at its prevailing market price by spreading the sale across several foreign markets. This approach allows the firms access to a larger amount of institutional and individual investors.

Summary

Any firm conducting international business uses international financial markets to facilitate their transactions, as summarized in Table 5.1. Most international business transactions are facilitated by the foreign exchange market. Transactions involving investments or financing in foreign currencies by the parent or subsidiaries are facilitated by the Eurocurrency, Eurocredit, Eurobond, and international stock markets. Each of these markets serves a particular financing need for MNCs. The Eurocurrency market facilitates short-term financing, while the Eurocredit market facilitates intermediate-term financing. Long-term debt financing is conducted through the Eurobond market, while long-term equity financing is conducted in international stock markets.

Table 5.1
Summary of International Financial Markets

International Financial Market	How the Market Is Used by the Parent or Subsidiaries
Foreign Exchange	• International transactions with customers from different countries • International investments • International financing
Eurocurrency Market	• International investing (deposits) in foreign currencies • Short-term financing in foreign currencies to support existing foreign operations
Eurocredit Market	• Intermediate-term financing in foreign currencies to support existing foreign expansion
Eurobond Market	• Long-term financing in foreign currencies to support foreign expansion
International Stock Markets	• Long-term financing

Discussion

The international business transactions of Jordan Co. are displayed in Figure 5.2.

(a) Explain the typical types of foreign exchange transactions that would be conducted by Jordan Co.

(b) Explain how the Eurocurrency and Eurocredit markets might be used by Jordan Co.

Figure 5.2
Illustration of Jordan's International Business

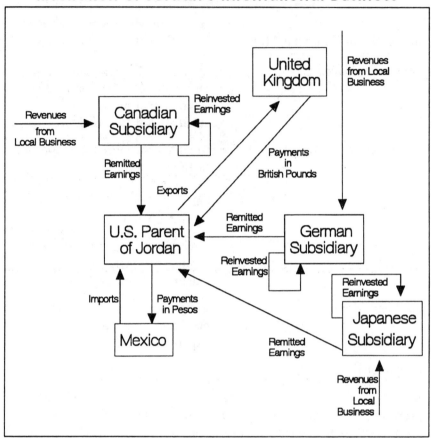

6

Risk and Return Tradeoffs in International Business

Some firms take more risk by engaging in projects that have the potential to generate higher returns. The term risk is used here to represent the uncertainty of net cash flows generated by the firm. The exposure to risk can sometimes be adjusted by firms, but there is a tradeoff between risk and return. This is especially true for international business transactions, in which there is exposure to economic conditions and exchange rate risk in foreign countries. An example is provided below.

Exposure to Foreign Economies

Consider a U.S. firm that distributes business calculators to retail book stores. It plans to expand into a foreign market, and is considering either Canada or New Zealand. It has developed projections of the average annual return on its investment for both alternatives based on three possible economic scenarios, as shown below:

| | **Average Annual Return on Investment Under:** | | |
	Very Favorable Economic Conditions	**Somewhat Favorable Economic Conditions**	**Unfavorable Economic Conditions**
Canada	20%	14%	2%
New Zealand	40%	20%	-9%

The investment in Canada has less risk because there is a well-established demand for business calculators, whereas the future interest in business calculators in New Zealand is not as clear. However, since many competitors are already distributing calculators to retail stores in Canada, the potential returns to the U.S. firm are somewhat limited. Conversely, there is very little competition for business calculators in New Zealand, because of somewhat stagnant business conditions there. The U.S. firm believes that if economic conditions improve in New Zealand, the popularity in business calculators will rise substantially, and the proposed project would generate high returns there. However, if New Zealand's business conditions are unfavorable, the project would generate a large loss.

Risk–Return Tradeoff

Put yourself in the firm's position. Should the firm prefer the Canadian project to the New Zealand project? The decision involves a risk–return tradeoff. The Canadian project can avoid the risk of a major loss, but it also forgoes the possibility of a very high return.

Assuming that each scenario has an equal probability of occurring, the expected return (E(r)) for each project is derived as:

Project	Expected Average Annual Return on Investment
Canadian	33.3% X 20% + 33.3% X 14% + 33.3% X 2% = 12%
New Zealand	33.3% X 40% + 33.3% X 20% + 33.3% X (-9%) = 17%

While the expected value of the return on investment is higher for New Zealand, the risk must also be considered because firms are risk averse. Since firms have different degrees of risk aversion, there will not be a unanimous preference in this example. Firms that have a high degree of risk aversion would prefer the Canadian project, while firms that have a low degree of risk aversion would prefer the New Zealand project.

Exposure to Exchange Rate Risk

Consider a U.S. firm that will receive 1 million French francs (FF) in one year as a result of exported products to a French business. When it receives the francs it will convert them to U.S. dollars. The U.S. firm can either attempt to benefit from its exposure to exchange rate risk or hedge the risk. Assume that the firm believes three possible scenarios could occur over the next year, each of which will result in a particular outcome for the value of the French franc in one year: (1) $.16, (2) $.21, or (3) $.24, each outcome having a probability of 33.3 percent. The cash inflows at the end of the year will be equal to 1 million francs times the value of the franc at that time.

Also assume that the cost of producing and sending the exports to the French firm is $170,000. The net cash flows resulting from the exports are equal to the cash inflows minus the outflows (taxes will be ignored in this example). But since the inflows are uncertain, the net cash flows are uncertain as well. The probability distribution of net cash flows is shown below:

Value of FF in One Year	Probability	Cash Inflows	Net Cash Flow
$.16	33.3%	$160,000	-$10,000
.21	33.3%	210,000	40,000
.24	33.3%	240,000	70,000

Hedging Exchange Rate Risk

The firm can attempt to hedge the exposure to exchange rate movements through the use of a forward contract, which is an agreement (with a commercial bank) to exchange one currency for another at a specified time and exchange rate. For our example, assume that a one year forward contract on francs has an exchange rate of $.20. The U.S. firm could engage in a forward contract to exchange its 1 million francs to be received one year from now into dollars, at $.20 per franc. Thus, the firm would receive $200,000 with certainty. This means that its net cash flows would be $30,000 with certainty (after deducting the cash outflow of $170,000).

Risk–Return Tradeoff

Put yourself in the firm's position. Would you hedge and lock in the net cash flows of $30,000 or remain unhedged? The first step before making your decision is to measure the expected value of the net cash flows (NCF) if you remain unhedged, which can be estimated as:

$$E(NCF) = \sum_{i=1}^{n} P_i NCF_i$$

where P_i represents the probability of a particular scenario and NCF_i represents the net cash flow that would occur under that scenario. In this example, there are three exchange rate scenarios, each scenario having a probability of 33.3 percent. The expected value of the NCF is:

$$
\begin{aligned}
E(NCF) \quad &= (33.3\% \times -\$10{,}000) \\
&\quad + (33.3\% \times \$40{,}000) \\
&\quad + (33.3\% \times \$70{,}000) \\
&= -\$3{,}333 \\
&\quad +\$13{,}333 \\
&\quad +\$23{,}333 \\
&= \ \$33{,}300
\end{aligned}
$$

Thus, the expected value of *NCF* when remaining unhedged is slightly higher than the $30,000 that would result from hedging.

The probability distribution of possible *NCF*s without hedging can be compared to the certain *NCF*, as illustrated in Figure 6.1. This figure

Figure 6.1
Probability Distribution of *NCF*s Without Hedging

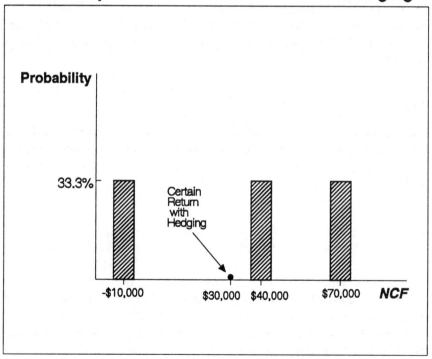

can be used to assess the tradeoff between expected return and risk when remaining unhedged. You may wish to consider explicitly the probability that remaining unhedged will result in a higher return than hedging. If you remain unhedged, you will enhance your return if the value of the franc in one year exceeds $.20. This will happen for two out of the three scenarios. Since each of these scenarios has a 33.3 percent chance of occurring, there is a 66.6 percent probability that by remaining unhedged you will enhance your return. However, under the other scenario that the franc is worth only $.16 in one year, the net cash flows would be -$10,000. There is a 33.3 percent chance that this will occur if you remain unhedged. Some firms may prefer to make sure they can avoid this scenario, even if it means accepting a lower expected return. There is no perfect solution to this dilemma. Those firms that are less averse to risk may be willing to remain unhedged. They will take the chance of incurring a loss in order to strive for higher returns.

Summary

These two examples show that firms engaged in international business commonly face a risk-return tradeoff. The financial decision under these circumstances will be based on the "magnitude" of the tradeoff, or the difference in possible returns, relative to the difference in risk between the alternative choices. The financial decision will also be influenced by the firm's attitude toward risk, since the perceived value of benefits from higher possible returns versus the perceived adverse effects of higher risk is dependent on the firm's degree of risk aversion.

Discussion

Jordan Company will be receiving one million British pounds in one year. It believes the pound's spot exchange rate will be either $1.70 (30 percent probability), $1.75 (50 percent probability), or $1.80 (20 percent probability), depending on economic conditions. It could use a forward contract to hedge the exports. The one-year forward rate is $1.73.

(a) Determine the probability distribution of dollars received if Jordan does not hedge.

(b) What is the expected value of the dollars to be received if Jordan does not hedge?

(c) What is the probability that Jordan will benefit from hedging?

(d) Should Jordan hedge? Explain.

7

International Risk and Return

Portfolio theory enables investors to understand how diversification may reduce risk. International diversification can be more effective than domestic diversification, as explained below. First, the portfolio theory is presented from the perspective of an investor in stocks (financial assets). Then, it is presented from the perspective of a corporation investing in real assets.

Investment in Financial Assets

The return on a portfolio of stocks is:

$$r_p = \sum_{i=1}^{n} w_i r_i$$

where:
  w_i = weight (proportion of total investment) allocated to the ith stock,

r_i = return generated from the ith stock,

n = number of stocks in the portfolio.

The risk of the portfolio is often measured as the variance of portfolio returns. For a two stock portfolio, the variance is:

$$\sigma_p^2 = w_A^2\sigma_A^2 + w_B^2\sigma_B^2 + 2w_Aw_B\sigma_{AB}$$

where w_A represents the weight assigned to stock A, w_B represents the weight assigned to stock B, σ_A^2 represents the variance of returns for stock A, σ_B^2 represents the variance of returns for stock B and σ_{AB} represents the covariance between stocks A and B. The formula illustrates how portfolio risk is a positive function of the variability of each stock's returns and the covariability between stock returns.

Reducing the Exposure of Financial Assets to U.S. Economic Conditions

Diversification across stocks can effectively reduce portfolio risk when the stocks are not highly correlated. Thus, the stocks will not likely experience poor performance at the same time. Under these conditions, the covariance term in the previous equation is low (or even negative), which results in a low σ_p^2 by including foreign stocks.

To illustrate the benefits from diversification, consider that as more stocks are added to a portfolio, the risk of the portfolio tends to decline. This is because stock returns are partially affected by firm-specific conditions. Since the returns are not perfectly correlated, diversification can reduce risk. After some point, the risk reduction resulting from the addition of more stocks is negligible. Since all U.S. stocks are systematically affected by general movements in the U.S. market, all risk cannot be diversified away. However, when including foreign stocks in the portfolio, risk can be reduced further (as shown in Figure 7.1), because the foreign stocks are systematically affected by their respective markets, and not so much by the U.S. market.

Figure 7.1
Potential Benefits From Domestic versus
International Diversification

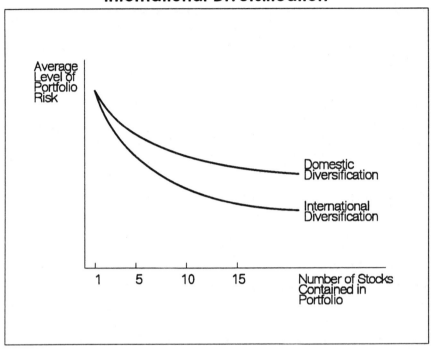

Reducing Exposure to Exchange Rate Risk

U.S. investors should be aware of the exchange rate risk resulting from investment in foreign stocks. If the currency denominating the foreign stocks depreciates against the dollar over the investment horizon, the return to the U.S. investor will be reduced. In some cases, the adverse exchange rate effects can more than offset any appreciation in the foreign stock itself, causing a negative return to a U.S. investor. Conversely, if the foreign currency strengthens against the dollar over the investment horizon, the return to the U.S. investor is enhanced by the exchange rate effects.

If U.S. investors wish to reduce the exchange rate risk on their investment in foreign stocks, they can use forward contracts or currency options to hedge their exposure. Alternatively, they can attempt to diversify their investment across foreign stocks in different countries. Using this strategy, the value of their foreign stock portfolio would be less sensitive to a substantial decline in one currency. However, diversification across countries whose currencies move together will not effectively reduce exchange rate risk. For example, most European currencies tend to move in the same direction against the dollar over time. Thus, if one European currency weakens against the dollar, all other European currencies would probably weaken as well. Consequently, diversification across European stocks does not effectively reduce the U.S. investor's exposure to exchange rate risk.

Investment in Real Assets

From a corporate perspective, the same portfolio concepts apply. Consider a U.S. corporation as a portfolio of business subsidiaries partitioned by type of product. For example, the return to a corporation with two business subsidiaries (called X and Y)

$$r = w_x r_x + w_y r_y$$

where w_x and w_y represent the weights assigned to business subsidiaries X and Y, while r_x and r_y represent the returns to the subsidiaries X and Y. The risk of the corporation may be measured as the variance of returns, or:

$$\sigma^2 = w_x^2 \sigma_x^2 + w_y^2 \sigma_y^2 + 2 w_x w_y \sigma_{xy}$$

The variance of returns to the corporation is positively related to the variance of returns for each business subsidiary, and the covariance of returns between subsidiaries.

Reducing the Exposure of Real Assets to U.S. Economic Conditions

If both subsidiaries are located in the U.S., they may be somewhat affected in a similar manner by U.S. economic conditions. However, if a corporation created a foreign subsidiary, that foreign subsidiary would likely be somewhat insulated from economic conditions in the corporation's home country. Consequently, the covariance of returns between the foreign subsidiary and U.S. subsidiary would be low, and the corporation's risk would be relatively low. To the extent that a corporation can reduce its risk through international diversification, it may be able to reduce the probability of failure. Consequently, it could achieve lower financing costs, as creditors would charge a lower risk premium because of the reduction in risk.

As the firm expands over time, it may consider entering other foreign countries whose economic conditions are not similar to those of the U.S. or to the one foreign country it has previously entered. The covariance of returns between a subsidiary established in a different country and its existing businesses should be low, because the performance of its subsidiaries are influenced by economic conditions in countries that are at least partially segmented from each other.

Reducing the Exposure of Real Assets to Exchange Rate Risk

Like U.S. investors in foreign financial assets, U.S. firms that invest in foreign real assets tend to benefit if the currencies denominating the assets appreciate against the dollar over time. The possible impact is not monitored as closely for real assets because the investment in real assets may be for 50 years or more. Nevertheless, if a U.S. firm is concerned about possible depreciation in the currencies denominating foreign real assets, it should consider diversifying its foreign investment across different countries whose currencies move somewhat independently of each other.

There are some obvious exceptions to the concept described above. A corporation would not necessarily reduce risk from diversifying its business internationally if it had no knowledge of international markets and customs. Also it may not reduce risk by creating a subsidiary in a less developed country with unstable political and economic conditions. Even though the covariance between returns of the subsidiary and a domestic subsidiary would be low, the variance of returns at this subsidiary might be very high. The net effect of this specific example might be increased risk of the corporation's portfolio of business operations.

Summary

Portfolio theory demonstrates how the diversification among assets that are not highly correlated can cause the portfolio's value to be much more stable than the values of its components. When viewing a U.S. firm as a portfolio of assets, the firm's performance overall should be more stable if the performance levels of its individual units (or subsidiaries) are not highly correlated. To the extent that the firm could achieve lower correlations among the performance levels of its individual subsidiaries by spreading its subsidiaries across countries with different economic conditions, it could possibly stabilize its performance overall. This implies that international diversification may reduce risk (defined here as volatility of performance) to a greater degree than domestic diversification.

Discussion

Jordan Co. has foreign subsidiaries in three different countries, exports supplies to the United Kingdom, and imports materials from Mexico. The annual return on assets (ROA, measured as net income divided by assets) was determined for the last ten years for all subsidiaries.

(a) Assume the standard deviation of the ROA over the last ten years was 3 percent for each foreign subsidiary. Do you think the standard deviation of Jordan's ROA from consolidated operations would be higher, lower, or equal to 3 percent? Why? (Ignore exchange rate effects when answering this question.)

(b) Assume the information in part (a), with this exception: Assume Jordan Co. did not have a German subsidiary and all foreign operations were conducted only by the Canadian and Japanese subsidiaries. Would the standard deviation of Jordan's ROA from consolidated operations be different than if there were three foreign subsidiaries? Explain.

8

Impact of International Business on Systematic Risk

Investors are presumed to be risk averse, which suggests that they prefer less risk to more, and would only be willing to incur more risk if they are compensated. The relationship between risk and the return required by investors is described below. Then, the impact of international investments on the risk and return of a portfolio is discussed.

Risk–Return Relationship

The so-called security market line (SML) expresses a linear positive relationship between the required rate of return on a firm's stock (called r) and the firm's level of systematic risk, as shown below:

$$r = R_f + (r_m - R_f)B$$

where R_f represents the risk–free rate, r_m represents the market return, and B represents the firm's beta (which is a measure of systematic risk). The firm's beta is estimated as the sensitivity of the firm's returns to market returns. A higher sensitivity is reflected in a higher beta, which implies a higher level of systematic risk. Investors will only invest in firms with higher systematic risk if the expected return is sufficiently high to compensate for the risk.

According to the security market line relationship, the return required by investors on the firm's stock would be lower if the firm could reduce its systematic risk. Some studies have found that firms with more international business have lower systematic risk. To the extent that firms affect their degree of systematic risk by engaging in international business, they could affect the required rate of return on their stock, and therefore reduce their cost of capital.

If investors could restructure the asset to reduce its sensitivity to the U.S. market (beta), without affecting the asset's expected return, its perceived value would increase. Assume the asset of concern is actually an asset portfolio, composed of many assets. If it is possible to restructure the composition of this asset portfolio to reduce its beta without affecting the expected return, the perceived value of this portfolio should increase.

Assume that all the assets in the portfolio are in the U.S., and therefore that their returns are systematically affected by the U.S. market. Also assume that some of these assets could be replaced with British assets, Canadian assets, and Japanese assets to achieve the same return for the entire portfolio. Would the asset portfolio beta be reduced?

Example

Is it really possible for a firm to significantly reduce its beta by engaging in international business? To answer this question, consider that a beta of a portfolio of assets is equal to the weighted average of the individual betas. Therefore, if a firm engages in international operations that represent 30 percent of the firm's total business, the beta of the firm's total business portfolio can be decomposed as:

$$B_p = \sum_{i=1}^{n} w_i B_i$$

where:

> w_i = weight (proportion of total investment) allocated to the ith asset,
>
> B_i = beta of the ith asset,
>
> n = number of assets in the portfolio.

If the U.S. assets have a beta ($B_{u.s.}$) of 1.2, international assets have a beta (B_g) of .2, the beta of the total business portfolio B is:

$$
\begin{aligned}
B_p &= w_{U.S.}B_{U.S.} + w_g B_g \\
&= .7(1.2) + .3(.2) \\
&= .9
\end{aligned}
$$

In this example, the firm is able to reduce its beta from 1.2 to .9 by engaging in international business.

The relationship between the firm's required rate of return and its beta is illustrated with a security market line (SML) in Figure 8.1. Assume that the firm's beta is estimated to be 1.2 if it does not engage in international business. The risk-free interest rate is 8 percent, and the expected market return is 12 percent.

Based on these assumptions, the firm's required rate of return is:

$$
\begin{aligned}
r &= R_f + (r_m - R_f)B \\
&= 8\% + (12\% - 8\%)1.2 \\
&= 8\% + 4.8\% \\
&= 12.8\%
\end{aligned}
$$

This required rate of return corresponds with the beta of 1.2 in Figure 8.1. If the firm engaged in international business and was able to reduce its beta to .9, its required rate of return (referred to as r') would now be:

$$
\begin{aligned}
r' &= R_f + (r_m - R_f)B \\
&= 8\% + (12\% - 8\%).9 \\
&= 8\% + 3.6\% \\
&= 11.6\%
\end{aligned}
$$

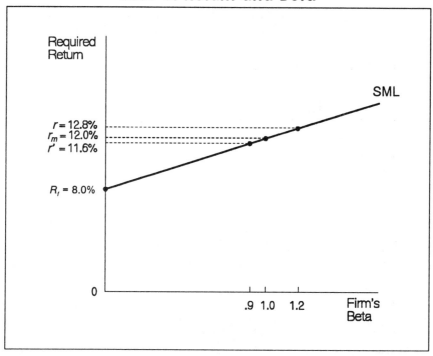

**Figure 8.1
Relationship Between Firm's Required
Rate of Return and Beta**

How International Business Affects Systematic Risk

By establishing business in foreign countries, a smaller proportion of the corporate performance is sensitive to its domestic country's economy. To the extent that the domestic market returns are driven by home economic conditions, the corporation's performance would now be less sensitive to the home market. This implies a lower degree of systematic risk.

Factors Affecting the Impact of International Business on Risk

The degree to which increased international business can reduce a firm's systematic risk is dependent on the following characteristics:

(1) Proportion of the firm's international business in relation to its total business.

(2) Location of international business.

(3) Exposure to exchange rate movements resulting from the international business.

Proportion of International Business/Total Business

The greater the proportion of a U.S. firm's international business, the less exposed it is to U.S. economic conditions, other things being equal.

Location of International Business

The potential reduction in risk resulting from increased international business can also be influenced by the location of international business. If the business is conducted in a country with similar economic conditions as the home country, this business would be indirectly sensitive to home economic conditions. Therefore, the corporation's level of systematic risk may not be reduced as much. U.S. firms that begin business in Canada, and European firms that cross over bordering countries may fit this description. The motives for these firms to conduct such international business is more likely focused on reasons other than reduction in systematic risk. Firms would more effectively reduce systematic risk by doing business in countries whose economies are somewhat segmented from those in their home countries.

Exchange Rate Movements

Exchange rate movements also must be considered when assessing how international business affects a firm's systematic risk. Some international business is highly influenced by exchange rates. For example, any U.S. exporting firms are affected when foreign currency values change against the U.S. dollar, since the demand for exports adjusts to changes in purchasing power. Even if economic conditions in the foreign countries were similar to the U.S. economy, the foreign demand for the exports may be most sensitive to exchange rate movements. As an example, the U.S. and foreign economies could be weak, causing weak U.S. demand for the U.S. corporation's products. Yet, the performance of the corporation's international business is influenced by the exchange rate effects, and is therefore somewhat insulated from the U.S. economy.

Type of International Business

The potential reduction in systematic risk may also be affected by the type of international business conducted by the corporation. Some types are reliant on home economic conditions and therefore could prevent the firms from reducing systematic risk. For example, consider a U.S. firm that developed a subsidiary in Mexico to produce goods that are exported back to the U.S. The sales by the subsidiary would likely be driven by the U.S. economy. Thus, the corporation's performance would still be very sensitive to the U.S. market.

Now consider a second type of international business, in which a U.S. firm begins a marketing campaign to export its product to Mexico. This exporting business would likely be affected by economic conditions in Mexico and the strength (or weakness) of the Mexican currency, the peso. Since the business is not likely to be very sensitive to the U.S. market conditions, the corporation's systematic risk may decline. The example illustrates how increased international business may allow for a decline in the systematic risk even if the business does not require the establishment of subsidiaries in foreign countries.

If the U.S. corporation described in the previous example established a campaign for exporting to Canada instead of Mexico, would there be as much potential for reducing the corporation's systematic risk? The answer depends on whether the Canadian exporting program would be more sensitive to the U.S. market conditions than the Mexican exporting program. The Canadian economic conditions are often similar to U.S. economic conditions. Therefore, the performance of the exporting program may be indirectly tied to U.S. market conditions. The exchange rate of the Canadian dollar also deserves to be considered, since the Canadian demand for exports is partially determined by the strength (or weakness) of the Canadian dollar. Since the Canadian dollar is very stable relative to the U.S. dollar, the performance of the Canadian exporting program is likely to be influenced mostly by the Canadian economy, and not by currency movements.

Summary

MNCs may be able to reduce their systematic risk by increasing their international business. However, the potential reduction in systematic risk is dependent on the location of the international business, sensitivity of the international business to exchange rate movements, and the type of international business conducted. An MNC is more likely to reduce its systematic risk if it engages in international business that is mostly influenced by factors unrelated to the domestic economy.

Discussion

Jordan Co. expected the performance of its foreign subsidiaries to be primarily dependent on the conditions in the host country and therefore somewhat insulated from U.S. conditions. Assume that each of Jordan's three foreign subsidiaries are the same size.

(a) Based on your knowledge of international conditions, which foreign subsidiary do you think would be most influenced by economic conditions in the U.S.?

(b) Jordan's products sold to British firms are produced by the U.S. parent. Does this imply that the performance resulting from its British business is primarily dependent on U.S. economic conditions? Explain.

9

International Asset Pricing

Investors and corporations use so-called asset pricing models such as the capital asset pricing model, (CAPM) to derive expected prices of assets. These models are based on the premise that the prices of some assets are systematically related to one or a few factors. The validity of a "foreign market factor" within an asset pricing model is dependent on the degree of segmentation between markets, as explained below.

Market Segmentation versus Integration

If each country's market was completely segmented from all other markets, the prices of assets (such as stocks) in that market should be insulated from conditions in other markets. Thus, the asset prices should be influenced solely by the conditions of their local market, and should not be systematically affected by foreign market conditions. With complete market segmentation, a local market index would serve as a reasonable proxy for the market variable in the capital asset pricing model. Asset prices in that market would be systematically influenced by the local market. Any movements in asset prices not caused by the local market would be caused by factors unique to the asset and would therefore reflect unsystematic risk.

At the other extreme, if all markets were completely integrated (no market segmentation), then asset prices would be systematically driven by a world index. In other words, markets would only be separate because of geography. If there were no barriers of any type, there would only be one worldwide market, and the local market would represent just a component of the world market.

In reality, there are barriers to international investment that can cause markets to be partially segmented. First, a lack of information about foreign assets could encourage investors to focus only on local investments. Second, transactions costs are commonly higher for international investments than local investments. Third, tax differentials between markets may discourage international investing. Fourth, most international investments require conversion to a foreign currency and are therefore exposed to exchange rate risk. The existence of such barriers causes markets to be partially segmented. With partial segmentation, prices of assets in a given market may be mostly driven by the conditions in that local market. However, since markets are not completely segmented, there can be some influence of foreign markets on local asset prices.

Tests of Global Market Segmentation

Since markets are not completely segmented, there is some question as to whether asset prices can be properly modeled using a single factor (the local market) in the capital asset pricing model (CAPM). This implies that the prices of assets are a function of two market forces: (1) the local market influence, and (2) the foreign market influence. Thus, returns on assets could be modeled with an international asset pricing model that captures the international market influence:

$$r_j = B_0 + B_1 r_m + B_2 r_f + e_j$$

where:

r_j = return on the jth asset
r_m = return on the local market
r_f = return on the foreign market
B_0 = constant

B_1 = sensitivity of the jth asset's returns to
the local market

B_2 = sensitivity of the jth asset's returns to the
foreign market

e_j = error term

A study by Agmon and Lessard[1] applied regression analysis to returns on U.S.-based multinational corporations to test whether there is a foreign market influence on the asset prices. They found that the regression coefficient B_2 was significant, which suggests that the foreign market is influential. However, there is some other evidence that suggests most of the systematic impact of market forces an asset prices comes from the local market. A study by Jorion and Schwartz[2] found that prices of Canadian stocks were highly influenced by the Canadian local market, but not by foreign markets.

The results of these two studies are not conflicting. The implications of Agmon and Lessard's study are that markets are not completely segmented, while the implications of Jorion and Schwartz's study are that markets are not completely integrated. Other studies have also empirically addressed this issue, without a clear consensus on whether an international asset pricing model is superior to the traditional one-factor CAPM.

Implications From Tests of Global Market Segmentation

Even though the international asset pricing issue is not completely resolved, some general implications can be extended. Since markets are not fully integrated, investors can possibly reduce their risk through international investing. The value of their overall portfolio may be

---

[1] Agmon, T. and D. Lessard, "Investor Recognition of Corporate International Diversification," *Journal of Finance*, September 1977, pp. 1049-55.

[2] Jorion, P. and F. Schwartz, "Integration vs Segmentation in the Canadian Stock Market," *Journal of Finance,* July 1986, pp. 602-16.

partially insulated from local market conditions when investing in foreign assets. This asset portfolio will likely be somewhat sensitive to specific foreign market conditions, but the sensitivity to any particular foreign market may be reduced by diversifying across foreign markets.

If all of these foreign assets were systematically influenced by the same global market conditions, the investor would not necessarily benefit from international diversification. All assets would be exposed to the systematic impact of the world index, and there would be no further risk reduction by spreading the investment across countries.

The degree to which all assets in a portfolio are influenced by similar global conditions is greater if the countries of the invested assets experienced similar economic patterns. For example, if part of a U.S. investor's asset portfolio was scattered across several European countries, the portfolio may be modeled as a function of the U.S. market and the European market. If most European countries experience similar economic cycles as the U.S., diversification across Europe will not effectively insulate the portfolio from systematic effects. A more effective form of diversification would be across continents.

If markets continue to become more integrated over time, asset prices will ultimately be driven by a world index rather than by the local markets where those assets are located. Yet, given that some formidable barriers to international investment still remain, investors can still capitalize on partially segmented markets.

Summary

To the extent that markets are segmented, U.S. investors may attempt to capitalize on conditions in foreign countries that differ from U.S. conditions. The term "investor" used in our discussion may be interpreted as an investor in "financial" assets, such as an individual investor or institutional investor. Alternatively, the term can also reflect a corporation that invests in "real" assets. In this case, the implications are focused on diversifying the corporation's real asset portfolio. The general principles hold for either perspective. However, the actual degree of segmentation between asset markets depends on the type (financial or real) of assets, since barriers between markets vary with the type of assets.

Discussion

Jordan Co. has noticed that the performance of its businesses in the U.S., Canada, Germany, and Japan are somewhat related.

(a) What does this suggest about the concept of market segmentation?

(b) Jordan Co. plans to set up a new large facility to sell medical supplies. Explain the effect on its domestic beta if the facility is established in the U.S., in Canada, or in New Zealand.

10

Stock Valuation of Multinational Corporations

Can the value of the stock of a multinational corporation (MNC) be determined in the same manner as that of a purely domestic stock? Yes and no! The procedure is the same, but the additional tasks are necessary. As with purely domestic firms, the value of an MNC is the present value of future cash flows. However, the characteristics of an MNC can complicate the estimation of discounted cash flows. Each subsidiary of an MNC has its own set of cash inflows and outflows, but these cash flows should not be double counted. Given that all the equity has been invested by the parent, the relevant cash flows are those associated with the parent. The expected cash flows resulting from earnings remitted by each subsidiary can be forecasted for each year. These estimated cash flows must then be converted to dollar cash flows at whatever exchange rate is expected to exist at that time.

Estimating an MNC's Cash Flows

Consider a U.S.-based MNC with a Canadian subsidiary, a German subsidiary, and a U.S. subsidiary. The cash flows received by the U.S. parent can be forecasted like any other domestic firm. However, the cash flows to be received by the parent from foreign operations require the following steps: (1) forecasting the cash flows generated by each subsidiary, (2) determining what proportion of those cash flows each subsidiary plans to remit to the parent, (3) deducting any withholding tax that must be paid by the subsidiary on remitted funds, and (4) forecasting the exchange rate at which the cash flows to be remitted will be converted into dollars. The forecasted dollar cash flows resulting from the different subsidiaries can be consolidated for each year, and then discounted to derive a present value of future cash flows.

Assume that the cash flows to be remitted by each of the three subsidiaries are as shown in Table 10.1 (after accounting for any taxes to

Table 10.1
Example of Estimating an
MNC's Cash Flows
(cash flows are in millions)

Canadian Subsidiary	Year 1	Year 2	Year 3
Forecasted funds to be remitted	C$700	C$700	C$900
Forecasted exchange rate	$.80	$.84	$.88
Forecasted dollar cash flows	$560	$588	$792
German Subsidiary			
Forecasted funds to be remitted	DM500	DM700	DM800
Forecasted exchange rate	$.60	$.64	$.62
Forecasted dollar cash flows	$300	$448	$496
U.S. Subsidiary			
Forecasted funds to be generated	$900	$1,000	$1,200

be paid). Since the funds to be remitted by the two foreign subsidiaries must be converted to dollars, forecasts for future exchange rates of the related currencies are provided. Only three years are shown in the table to simplify the example. This process would have to be repeated for all future years.

The discount rate applied to cash flows remitted by the subsidiaries may vary among subsidiaries, since the risk of each subsidiary is unique. Alternatively, the future cash flows of each subsidiary could be adjusted for risk, which would allow the cash flows across subsidiaries to be discounted at a similar discount rate.

By reviewing the table, it should be obvious why the subsidiary cash flows not remitted to the parent are excluded from the analysis. Those cash flows are reinvested by the subsidiary to generate future cash flows. When these future cash flows are remitted to the parent, they will be included at that time. If they were also counted when they were reinvested by the subsidiary, they would have been counted twice. They should only be counted at the time at which they are to be received by the parent.

Recall that the value of the firm is equal to the value of its equity plus the value of its debt. Thus, the equity value can be determined by subtracting the value of debt from the total value of the firm. Then, the equity value of the firm is divided by the number of shares outstanding to determine the proper value per share.

Limitations of Estimating Cash Flows

Some of the estimates necessary to derive the MNC's value are subject to error. In our example, the estimates of cash flows to be remitted by the subsidiaries may be incorrect, because of errors in forecasting their sales, expenses, or taxes. Even the U.S. subsidiary's forecasted cash flows are subject to error.

Since future exchange rates are uncertain, the dollar cash flows resulting from remittances by foreign subsidiaries are uncertain. Thus, even if the level of foreign cash flows to be remitted is accurately estimated, the dollars they will convert to is subject to error.

If an MNC used all possible information, it would still be unable to derive perfectly accurate estimates of future cash flows. Investors or other firms that wish to determine the proper value of the MNC will experience more severe estimation problems, because much of the information needed about the firm (such as detailed plans of future restructuring) is not disclosed to the public.

Expected Dividend Model

Given the limited information available to use a discounted cash flow method for valuing an MNC, alternative methods should be considered. One alternative valuation method is to apply the expected dividend model. If investors plan to maintain a common stock forever, the expected cash flows of the stock are its dividends. The value of the common stock could be determined as:

$$V_s = \frac{D_1}{(1+k)^1} + \frac{D_2}{(1+k)^2} + \ldots$$

where D represents the dividend paid, k represents the required rate of return on the stock, and the subscripts represent the periods of concern.

Since future dividends paid by the parent of an MNC are influenced by the parent's cash flows, it may still be necessary to estimate the cash flows that will be remitted by each subsidiary. Since the underlying information used to derive estimates in the expected dividend model is subject to much uncertainty, the proper value of the firm's stock is still difficult to estimate.

Impact of Exchange Rates on an MNC's Value

Since an MNC's cash flows are affected by exchange rate movements, its value is affected as well. The cash flows are usually affected either from international trade transactions, or from funds remitted by foreign subsidiaries, as described below.

Impact on MNC's International Trade Transactions

U.S. exporting firms tend to benefit when the dollar weakens, because the amount of foreign currency needed to purchase dollar–denominated goods is reduced. Thus, foreign demand for the goods is increased, which results in increased cash flows. If the goods exported by the U.S. firm were denominated in the foreign currency, the U.S. firm still benefits when the dollar weakens because the proceeds from the exports convert to more dollars, resulting in increased cash flows. The opposite effects should occur when the dollar strengthens against foreign currencies.

The suggested impact of exchange rates on U.S.-based MNCs is based on the assumption that other factors are held constant. Since these factors are not constant in reality, the impact of exchange rates is not always obvious. Reconsider a U.S. exporter of dollar–denominated goods. If the dollar weakens, it was suggested that foreign demand for the goods would increase. However, some competitors in those foreign countries may reduce their price (and therefore profit margin) to retain their market share. Under these conditions, the U.S. firm will not necessarily experience an increased demand for its goods, even though the dollar weakened. Thus, the dollar cash flows may not be affected.

Even if competitors do not adjust their price, it is possible that the economic conditions that led to a change in the value of the dollar will affect the U.S. firm in an offsetting way. For example, if relatively high U.S. inflation caused the weak dollar, it could also increase the relative cost of producing goods in the U.S. Therefore, the U.S. firm may need to increase its prices to cover the higher cost. While the foreign customers can obtain more dollars with a given amount of foreign currency when the dollar weakens, it now takes more dollars to purchase the goods from the U.S. firm. If the actual purchasing power of the foreign customers does not increase because of the possible offsetting effect described here, the demand for foreign goods may not be affected by a weakened dollar. This example is based on the concept of purchasing power parity, which suggests that exchange rates will adjust to inflation differentials, so that the relative purchasing power of foreign goods versus local goods is retained.

While the dollar's value is sensitive to inflationary changes in the U.S. versus other countries, it rarely adjusts in a manner that perfectly offsets the differential inflation rates. Since there are other factors in addition to inflation that affect the dollar's value, the offsetting effect described above is unlikely. Nevertheless, there may be a partial offsetting effect in some cases.

Impact on Earnings Remitted by Foreign Subsidiaries

Since the dollar cash flows resulting from a given amount of earnings remitted by foreign subsidiaries is affected by the prevailing exchange rate, the MNC's value is affected as well. Specifically, a weakening dollar increases the dollar cash flows resulting from a given level of remitted foreign earnings, and therefore should increase the value of the MNC.

Conversely, a stronger dollar reduces the dollar cash flows resulting from a given level of remitted earnings and therefore should reduce the value of an MNC. This can be confirmed by looking back at the Canadian subsidiary's position in Table 10.1. In Years 1 and 2, the Canadian subsidiary was expected to remit C$700 million. In Year 1, the remitted funds were expected to convert to $560 million, based on an exchange rate of $.80 per Canadian dollar. However, in Year 2, the same amount of remitted funds were expected to convert to $588 million, ($28 million more than before), based on an expected exchange rate of $.84 for that time period. In this example, the Canadian dollar was expected to strengthen by 5 percent, so that the given level of remitted Canadian dollars converts to a 5 percent increase in the U.S. dollars to be received. Thus, the expected weakening of the U.S. dollar causes an increase in expected dollar cash flows.

The relationship between the value of the dollar and the value of the MNC can be distorted because cash flow streams within MNCs are not necessarily in one direction. While foreign subsidiaries periodically remit earnings to the U.S. parent, the parent may sometimes invest its own funds in foreign subsidiaries to support expansion. The parent may also purchase foreign supplies or materials, which causes an exchange of dollars for foreign currencies. Under such circumstances, a weakened dollar could increase dollar outflows and therefore reduce the parent's net cash flows, while a strengthened dollar would have the opposite effect.

Summary

The valuation of a firm involves determining the present value of the MNC's future cash flows. This present value can be used to value shares of stock given the number of shares of stock outstanding. This valuation process can be applied to domestic firms and MNCs. However, the process is more complex when valuing MNCs, because future cash flows of MNCs are dependent on financial conditions of the countries where the MNCs do business. Since these characteristics are difficult to forecast, cash flow projections of MNCs are subject to much uncertainty. Nevertheless, analysts should at least be able to use their forecasts of international conditions to determine whether an MNC's value will rise or decline in the future.

Discussion

Jordan Co. periodically exports medical supplies to the United Kingdom. Their main competition in the British market is from various French firms that export franc-denominated supplies to British customers, and from some British firms. Assume that the British pound is expected to appreciate against the French franc and remain stable against the dollar.

(a) Given that the pound/dollar exchange rate is expected to be stable, Jordan's export business with British customers should not be affected by any exchange rate movements. Do you agree?

(b) If the pound depreciated substantially against the franc and depreciated slightly against the dollar, how do you think Jordan's value would be affected?

11

Valuation of Foreign Stock

The value of a common stock represents the present value of the expected cash flows generated by that stock. The perceived value may vary with the way in which expected cash flows are measured. Various models are available for measuring the expected cash flows. Conceptually, foreign stocks are also valued as the present value of expected cash flows. However, since foreign stocks are denominated in foreign currencies, an exchange rate adjustment is necessary. This adjustment is illustrated for each of the models commonly used for stock valuation.

Expected Dividend Model

For investors who plan to maintain a common stock forever, the expected cash flows of the stock are its dividends. Thus, the value of the common stock is:

$$V_s = \frac{D_1}{(1 + k)^1} + \frac{D_2}{(1 + k)^2} + \ldots$$

where D represents the dividend paid, k represents the required rate of return on the stock, and the subscripts represent the periods of concern.

The value of a foreign common stock (V_f) can be measured in the same way after including an adjustment for exchange rate effects:

$$V_f = \frac{D_1 \times E_1}{(1 + k)^1} + \frac{D_2 \times E_2}{(1 + k)^2} + \ldots$$

where E represents the value of the foreign currency denominating the foreign stock. This model converts the dividends paid in foreign currency to the local investor's home currency in each period.

The model for V_f demonstrates how the perceived value of a foreign stock is increased (reduced) when the foreign currency denominating the stock is expected to appreciate (depreciate) against the local currency.

There is uncertainty in both the domestic model and the foreign model because future dividends are unknown. However, there is more uncertainty in the foreign model because of the exchange rate variable, which is also unknown. In fact, exchange rates tend to be much more volatile than corporate dividends.

Zero Growth Dividend Model

For common stocks paying a dividend of D that are expected to have zero dividend growth, the domestic model can be written as:

$$V_s = \frac{D}{(1 + k)^1} + \frac{D}{(1 + k)^2} + \ldots$$

Since D is a constant amount and is paid to infinity, this model reflects the present value of a perpetuity, or:

$$V_s = \frac{D}{k}$$

The foreign model for the value of a common stock (V_f) with zero dividend growth is:

$$V_f = \frac{D \times E_1}{(1 + k)^1} + \frac{D \times E_2}{(1 + k)^2} + \ldots$$

The model cannot be simplified to the present value of a perpetuity because the expected cash flow in each period varies with the exchange rate. An exception is when a specified exchange rate (called E) is used as the forecast for every future period, in which case the foreign model can be described as:

$$V_f = \frac{D \times E}{(1 + k)^1} + \frac{D \times E}{(1 + k)^2} + \ldots$$

Constant Rate of Growth

For common stocks that are paying a dividend of D and are expected to exhibit a constant dividend growth rate of g, the domestic value is:

$$V_s = \frac{D_0(1 + g)}{k - g} = \frac{D_1}{k - g}$$

This formula is derived in many financial management textbooks.

Foreign stocks that pay dividends according to a constant growth rate cannot be valued in this simplified manner because of exchange rate effects.

Implications of Valuation Models Applied to a Foreign Stock

If the prevailing exchange rate is used as a forecast of exchange rates for all future periods, and outside investors have the same dividend expectations as local investors, the valuation of common stock may not be any different for outside investors than local investors (assuming no tax differentials). However, one might argue that under these conditions, the outside investors would value the common stock lower than local investors for the following reasons. First, there are higher costs (or inconveniences) associated with monitoring the stock of a foreign company. Second, outside investors may incur transactions costs from exchanging the foreign dividend payments into their home currency. Third, even though expected cash flows are the same, these cash flows are more uncertain because of exchange rate effects. If outside investors require a higher rate of return on the stock, the cash flows would be discounted at a higher rate.

Regardless of the model used, investors are more likely to believe a foreign stock is undervalued when they anticipate that the foreign currency of concern will strengthen. Even if local investors and outside investors of a specific country have the same exact expectations for a common stock's future dividends, they may have different perceptions of the stock's value because of exchange rate effects.

Another factor that can cause perceptions between local and outside investors to vary is the tax liability. Local investors may be subject to a different tax code than outside investors. Thus, even if both types of investors had the same dividend expectations and the exchange rate was expected to be stable, after-tax cash flows generated by the stock could vary among investors.

Valuation of Stocks in New Markets

In recent years, stock markets have been created in some less developed countries in Latin America, the Pacific Basin, and in Eastern Europe. The growth of these markets followed the mass privatization programs initiated by the respective national governments. For example, governments in Argentina, Czechoslovakia, Hungary, Mexico, and Poland are selling numerous business related assets that were previously "state-owned" to individuals. As a result, publicly held corporations are created. Since owners of the shares of these corporations may desire to sell their shares, a secondary market for stocks is necessary. In Czechoslovakia, it is estimated that up to 2,000 firms will have publicly traded shares once their privatization program is completed.

The creation of many new foreign stocks is of interest to U.S. investors. In the late 1980s and the early 1990s, some U.S. investors experienced large gains from investing in mutual funds (stock portfolios managed by investment companies) representing markets such as Hong Kong, Malaysia, Spain, and Thailand. From 1989 through 1991, each separate mutual fund focusing on these markets experienced returns of over 100 percent for U.S. investors.

Given the performance of stocks in these markets, many U.S. investors desire to assess the value of firms that have recently been privatized. Yet, there are some limitations of valuing such firms, for the following reasons. First, the previous financial performance of the firm may be unknown, because financial statements were not available before the firm was privatized. Second, when the firm was state-owned, it did not operate under goals of maximizing the value of the stock, since stock did not even exist. Past performance of a state-owned firm is not a useful indicator of future performance following the privatization process.

Overall, there is very little information available to estimate the cash flows of firms in these markets, or to estimate the risk when developing a required rate of return from investing in these firms. Furthermore, the future exchange rate of the local currency against the dollar is very uncertain.

Overall, information on the key aspects needed to properly value cash flows of these foreign stocks is unavailable. Yet, some investors may perceive the lack of information as an advantage. The lack of information about the stocks serves as a barrier to some investors. Those U.S. investors who are willing to use crude estimates for their valuations may identify firms that they believe are highly undervalued. There is a greater likelihood of finding undervalued stocks when information is not complete, because a more comprehensive analysis by numerous investment analysts is not possible.

As time passes and more financial information becomes available, investment analysts will be able to more properly value the stock and capitalize on any market inefficiencies. These actions will force market prices of the stocks to gravitate toward their proper levels, and therefore remove the inefficiencies. Investors who wait until such information is available before investing in these stocks can reduce their risk, but also reduce their chances of benefiting from market inefficiencies.

Perspective of a Potential Acquirer

Up to this point, the discussion has been presented from the perspective of an individual or institutional investor in the U.S. When using the perspective of a U.S. corporation that is performing the valuation for purposes of acquiring the foreign firm, several adjustments are necessary in the valuation procedure. The most obvious adjustment is that if a U.S. firm acquires the foreign firm, the operations of the foreign firm may be restructured, and so may the cash flows. The value of the foreign firm from the perspective of the U.S. firm can be measured as the present value of future cash flows remitted by the foreign firm to the U.S. firm. To estimate the present value from this perspective, the U.S. firm would have to perform the following tasks in this order:

(1) Consider how it would restructure the foreign firm's operations, if at all.

(2) Estimate the cash flows to be generated by the foreign firm over time.

(3) Determine what proportion of the cash flows generated should be reinvested by the foreign subsidiary versus the proportion of cash flows the subsidiary should remit to the U.S. firm.

(4) Based on tasks (2) and (3), estimate the amount of cash flows (after taxes) that will be remitted to the U.S. firm.

(5) Estimate the exchange rate of the foreign firm's local currency with respect to the dollar in future periods.

(6) Using estimates from tasks (4) and (5) estimate the dollar cash flows (and adjust for any tax effects in the U.S.) to be received by the U.S. firm in each future period.

(7) Discount these dollar cash flows using a required rate of return on this investment (the acquisition) to obtain an estimated present value of the foreign firm.

(8) If the U.S. firm will assume any debt of the foreign firm, it can deduct the value of this debt to determine the value of the foreign firm's equity. If no foreign debt is to be assumed, the present value of the foreign firm reflects the value of that firm's equity.

The tasks outlined above can be performed to estimate the equity value of the foreign firm. If the U.S. firm is able to purchase the foreign firm for an amount less than its estimated value, it would pursue the acquisition. If the purchase price of the foreign firm exceeds its estimated value, the acquisition is not worth pursuing.

Summary

Whether the U.S. investor is an individual purchasing some shares of a foreign firm or a corporation that wishes to purchase all the shares of the foreign firm (acquisition), the investor should estimate the equity value of the foreign firm. This equity value can be compared to the prevailing market value of the firm's equity to determine whether the foreign firm is undervalued, and therefore whether to invest in the firm. The valuation procedure will normally be conducted more thoroughly by a potential acquirer than an individual investor because the amount to be invested is much larger. In addition, the potential acquirer can influence the foreign firm's future cash flows through restructuring, whereas the individual investor has no direct influence over the foreign firm.

Discussion

The U.S. parent of Jordan Company is considering an investment in 70 percent of all the shares of a French firm that produces medical supplies and sells them locally. The French firm would periodically send dividend payments to the U.S. parent of Jordan Company. The executives of Jordan are presently attempting to value the French firm from their perspective.

(a) Would the perceived value of the French firm from Jordan's perspective be enhanced or reduced by anticipated depreciation of the French franc over the next several years?

(b) Based on the forecast of the French franc as stated in part (a), should Jordan act immediately to make the purchase or defer the purchase until a future point in time?

12

Valuation of International Bonds

As financial markets become more globally integrated, investors have easier access to money market securities, stocks, or bonds that are sold in foreign countries. Investors with long-term funds available may be interested in international bonds offered outside the U.S. International bonds can be classified as either foreign bonds or Eurobonds. Foreign bonds are issued by an issuer foreign to where the bonds are sold. Eurobonds are sold in countries other than the country represented by the currency denominating them.

International bonds sometimes offer a higher yield than local bonds. However, there are some risks to consider as well. To understand how international bonds vary from bonds issued locally in the local currency, the valuation of bonds must be understood. The differences in the valuation of an international bond versus a U.S. bond from the perspective of U.S. investors can help illustrate the potential reward and risk from investing in an international bond.

Valuation of a U.S. Bond

The value of a bond represents the present value of the expected cash flows generated by that bond. Investors who hold bonds until maturity receive cash flows in two forms: interest payments, and maturity (or par) value. The present value of a bond (V_b) can be measured as:

$$V_b = \sum_{t=1}^{m} \frac{I_t}{(1 + k)^t} + \frac{M}{(1 + k)^m}$$

where I_t represents the coupon paid at the end of each period, M represents the principal payment made at maturity, k represents the required rate of return by investors, t represents the period of concern, and m represents the number of periods until maturity.

Valuation of International Bonds From a U.S. Perspective

International bonds are issued by firms from many different countries and are denominated in a variety of currencies. The valuation of dollar-denominated bonds by U.S. investors can be performed using the equation above, regardless of the country in which they are placed. However, the valuation of other bonds by U.S. investors must account for exchange rate movements. The present value of an international bond can be written as:

$$V_b^* = \sum_{t=1}^{m} \frac{I_t \times E_t}{(1 + k)^t} + \frac{M \times E_m}{(1 + k)^m}$$

where E represents the exchange rate of the foreign currency denominating the bond with respect to the investor's currency. For U.S. investors, E reflects the value of the foreign currency with respect to the dollar.

This model converts the interest and par value payments to the investor's home currency in each period. Tax effects are not accounted for here.

Impact of Exchange Rate Movements

The model for V_b^* demonstrates how the perceived value of a foreign bond is increased (reduced) when the foreign currency denominating the bond is expected to appreciate (depreciate) against the investor's currency. While the interest rate payments and par value are known with certainty (assuming the issuer does not default), future exchange rates are subject to much uncertainty.

Some bonds sold in foreign countries are denominated in U.S. dollars. These bonds may be issued by foreign firms that need dollars to support their U.S. operations. The bonds may be more easily sold outside the U.S. if the issuing firms have more name recognition there. Some dollar-denominated bonds sold in foreign countries are issued by U.S. firms. These firms may use the Eurobond market to place bonds in countries where they are attempting to build name recognition. In addition, they may believe that they can reduce their transactions costs by selling bonds in foreign countries, as fees changed by investment banks for placing an issuer's bonds can vary among regions.

Bonds denominated in dollars and sold in foreign countries will be valued by U.S. investors in a manner similar to bonds issued in the U.S., since exchange rates are not a factor. However, there may be different tax effects under some circumstances.

Impact of Foreign Interest Rate Movements

When bonds are sold before maturity, the cash flows to the investors are coupon payments up to the time of sale and the price at which the bond was sold. The selling price of the bond is inversely related to interest rate movements in the foreign country of concern, because the required rate of return by prospective investors is influenced by interest rate movements in that country. If interest rates decline over time, investors in that country will be willing to pay a higher price for bonds that were previously issued when the coupon rates were higher. Thus, international bonds may be especially attractive when interest rates in the foreign country are expected to decline over the investment horizon.

Other Factors to Consider

If the present exchange rate is used as a forecast of future exchange rates (which implies no change in the exchange rate), the valuation of the bond from the perspective of investors within the country may be similar to the valuation by investors outside the country. However, there are conditions in which the valuation by investors within the country may differ from the valuation by investors outside the country. First, the credit risk perception of the bond by the two types of investors may vary, causing investors inside the country to incorporate a different credit risk premium in their required rate of return than that used by investors outside the country.

Second, even if the issuer's credit risk is perceived the same across investors, those investors outside the country may incorporate an extra risk premium to account for exchange rate risk resulting from coupon payment to be received in the form of a foreign currency. Third, the tax effects may vary with the investor's home country, causing different after-tax cash flows for investors inside the country than investors outside the country. Fourth, the costs of monitoring the bond may be higher for investors outside the country, which could reduce the perceived value from their perspective. Fifth, investors outside the country may incur transaction costs from the conversion of interest payments to their home currency, which could reduce the perceived value from their perspective.

Floating-Rate International Bonds

Many bonds in countries outside the U.S. have floating coupon rates that are tied to local market interest rates. That is, the coupon rate changes every year or so, depending on the prevailing market interest rates of the currency denominating the bond. This feature is distinctly different from the bonds with fixed coupon rates that are common in the U.S. Floating-rate bonds can have a favorable effect on the yield earned by investors if market interest rates rise. However, they can have an unfavorable effect on the yield to investors if interest rates decline. Furthermore, the cash flows from floating-rate bonds are subject to more uncertainty (even for investors not exposed to exchange rate risk), because the coupon payment is not known. U.S. investors who purchase floating-rate bonds must attempt to forecast future interest rates of the currency denominating the bond to estimate the future cash flows to be received from the bond.

International Bonds Issued by U.S. Firms

While international bonds can attract U.S. investors when favorable exchange rate and interest rate movements are expected, the lack of information about these bonds can discourage investment by the U.S. investors. Some recent developments reduce this type of barrier to international investment. Information about the financial condition of the foreign firms issuing the bonds can be obtained. Alternatively, U.S. investors could focus on international bonds issued by U.S. companies to finance their foreign operations. Investors may be able to obtain more information to assess the financial condition of these firms.

Summary

International bonds can be attractive to U.S. investors when (1) they offer a higher coupon rate than U.S. bonds, and (2) the currency denominating these bonds is expected to appreciate against the dollar. If the bond has a fixed interest payment and interest rates in the foreign country of concern are expected to decline, this is an additional advantage, since these would be in demand in the secondary market in the future. (Floating-rate bonds are generally more appealing when interest rates in that country are expected to rise.) However, even with these possible advantages, investors must recognize the possible risks associated with investing in international bonds.

Discussion

The German subsidiary of Jordan Co. has issued bonds with a fixed coupon rate and denominated in marks to finance operations there. The bonds can be purchased and resold in various European markets.

(a) Assume that you expect U.S. interest rates to increase, and German interest rates to decrease. Explain how the value of bonds issued by Jordan's subsidiary would be affected over time.

(b) Assume that you expect the mark to appreciate against the dollar consistently over time. As a U.S. investor, explain how this would affect your dollar cash inflows received from the bond.

13

Global Market Efficiency

Market efficiency implies that security prices reflect all information. There are different levels of efficiency, each level based on specific type of information. Weak-form efficiency suggests that security prices reflect all stock price and volume information. In other words, investors would not be able to achieve excess risk-adjusted returns by employing a trading strategy that is based on recent price patterns of particular stocks. Semistrong-form efficiency suggests that security prices reflect all publicly available information, including any corporate announcements. Strong-form efficiency suggests that security prices reflect all public and inside information. Based on numerous empirical studies, there is some support for weak-form and semistrong-form efficiency in the U.S., but there is evidence refuting strong-form efficiency. This implies that the only way to consistently achieve excess risk-adjusted returns is to have access to inside information (although trading on such information is illegal).

Market Efficiency
in Foreign Markets

Market efficiency has not received as much attention in non–U.S. markets since many of those markets are not as developed. However, as U.S. investors have easier access to foreign markets, curiosity about possible inefficiencies in these markets has increased.

Some foreign markets are more prone to inefficiencies because of country characteristics. The financial statements required of firms are less standardized, causing less comparability among financial statements. This may give an advantage to investors who conduct research to closely analyze the financial conditions of firms. The lack of standardization can essentially serve as an information barrier that creates an advantage for those investors that can circumvent it.

Rules on insider trading tend to be less restrictive in non–U.S. markets. Thus, there may be more opportunities to legally benefit from insider trading in these markets. U.S. investors will not necessarily capitalize on these opportunities because they will not have inside information on foreign firms. In fact, they may have trouble obtaining adequate public information about these firms.

Impact of High Inflation
on Stock Markets

If the returns on each stock market are measured in terms of the local currency over a time, the stock markets in less developed countries (LDCs) would likely show the highest returns. Does this mean that there is a global inefficiency which investors (including those from the U.S.) can capitalize on? Not necessarily! First, there may be restrictions that prohibit foreign investment in these markets. But even if there are no restrictions, the investors from the U.S. and elsewhere will not necessarily benefit. To understand why, consider that the local investors will only invest in stocks that are expected to meet their required return, which is mainly composed of two parts: (1) the local risk-free rate, and (2) the risk premium. Since investors could easily earn the local risk-free rate of return by investing in local treasury securities, they should expect at least such a return from stocks. Yet, a risk premium is also necessary because the stocks exhibit risk. The required rate of return on stocks of LDCs will normally be very high because the risk-free rate in these countries is so high. Given the high expected inflation that exists in these countries, the annual risk-free interest rate often exceeds 30 percent. Furthermore, since the stocks traded in these countries tend to be volatile, a high risk premium is required. So the required rate of return on stocks in LDCs may exceed 60 percent.

If U.S. investors invested in these stocks, their returns would typically be much lower. While the high inflation in LDCs boosts the required rate of return by their local investors, it also tends to cause severe depreciation of their currencies against those of industrialized countries (such as the U.S.). Thus, after U.S. investors purchase stocks of these countries, the currency denominating the stocks depreciates against the U.S. dollar. By the time U.S. investors sell the stock and convert the proceeds to dollars, the foreign currency has depreciated substantially against the dollar, thereby offsetting much of the stock price appreciation. These currencies sometimes depreciate against the dollar by 60 percent or more per year.

Only the local investors of LDCs can benefit from the high stock price appreciation, without being directly exposed to their home currency's weakness. However, they are not necessarily increasing their purchasing power, since the large gains in stock prices may even be less than the inflation rate. In summary, differential gains across stock markets does not imply that some markets are improperly priced. Exchange rate movements and country specific characteristics must be accounted for when comparing stock performance across markets.

Inefficiencies in New Markets

Stock markets are more likely to have inefficiencies if they have existed for only a short period of time. As time passes, investors tend to capitalize on any inefficiencies, which pushes stock prices toward their proper levels. In the established stock markets such as the U.S., there are numerous investment analysts and advisers who search for undervalued stocks. Given the attention given to valuation of stocks in these markets, it is somewhat difficult to find any blatant inefficiencies. However, in markets that were recently developed, the stocks have not been analyzed as closely, and therefore may be improperly priced. Any inefficiencies should be reduced when more financial information about the corporations becomes publicly available.

In recent years, many businesses in Eastern Europe and Latin America that were previously owned by the national governments were privatized, thereby transferring ownership from the government to investors. In may cases, the stock owned by investors is publicly traded, which has resulted in the development of stock markets in these countries. The privatization of government owned businesses requires a valuation of the shares to be distributed (sold) to shareholders. This process is normally facilitated by comparison of the firm's operations to other firms in the same industry whose shares are publicly traded. For example, if shares of the publicly traded firms in the industry have a price-earnings ratio (price per share of stock divided by earnings per share) of 8, then the firm that is privatized could be valued as 8 times its recent earnings. (There are some limitations of this valuation process, but the simple example used here is sufficient to make a point.) However, in a country where market prices of shares are not available, one could not apply an industry price-earnings ratio. There is no benchmark for comparison purposes.

An alternative approach for determining the market value of a firm is to estimate the market value of the assets as if the firm was going to liquidate the assets, then subtract any existing debt, and divide the remaining value (the so-called liquidation value) by the number of existing shares. However, the market values of individual assets is difficult to estimate in an economy where prices were previously set by the government.

A third valuation procedure would be to estimate future cash flows of the firm and discount them at the required rate of return. This present value could be divided by the number of shares to derive a price per share of stock. However, the estimation of cash flows requires anticipated expenses, which are based on prices of materials, leasing, wages, machinery, etc. Historical data on expenses while the firms were owned by the government can not be used to develop estimates because prices were set by the government. As these countries adopt a free enterprise system, prices are market determined. Another component of cash flow is revenue, which will be affected by pricing and the level of competition. In the past, competition was controlled by the government.

Given the movement away from government control, the valuation of the firm by using estimated cash flows or any other means is subject to much uncertainty. Thus, there may be many undervalued stocks in these countries. As land costs and wages gravitate toward some equilibrium, and the level of competition becomes more clear, expenses and revenue should be more predictable, and the valuations should be more accurate.

Stock markets in Eastern Europe and Latin America are subject to inefficiencies because the information necessary to estimate costs, revenue, or the market value of assets may be limited to some investors. Those investors who have access to information (perhaps through government agencies or other sources) may be able to capitalize on the inefficiencies. As more financial information becomes available and accessible to all investors, stock prices will more properly reflect firm value, and market inefficiencies will be reduced.

Capitalizing on Undervalued Stock Markets

As foreign stock markets become more accessible, some investors attempt to determine whether an entire stock market is overpriced or underpriced. Two of the more obvious ways of capitalizing on an undervalued stock market are: (1) buy an international mutual fund that is composed of stocks from that country, or (2) buy futures contracts on a stock index representing that country (these contracts lock in the price paid for the index, so that if the index rises, investors earn the difference between the existing price and the futures price as of a specified future date). Investors can capitalize on an overvalued stock market by selling futures contracts on that market. Futures contracts on various stock markets will likely be developed over time.

Many analysts have claimed that Japanese stocks were overpriced throughout the 1980s, because the multiples of the firm's stock price per share to earnings per share were typically much higher than firms of other countries. Since the price of the stock should possibly reflect a multiple of recent earnings, a high multiple implies that the firm's stock is priced higher than it should be. These concerns about overvalued firms may have even led to the severe decline in Japanese stock prices in the early

1990s. However, one must be cautious when comparing stock prices across firms in different countries. Accounting standards differ substantially across countries, so that reported earnings per share of firms in different countries may not be comparable. Therefore, it is dangerous to apply common price-earnings multiples from any U.S. industry to a Japanese firm's earnings in order to derive an appropriate stock price for the firm. Firms in different countries also have different degrees of financial leverage, which can cause earnings per share differentials across countries.

The performance among stock markets varies over any period assessed. For example, over the first five and one-half months of 1992, Hong Kong and Mexican stock prices appreciated by over 29 percent, while the U.S. stock prices declined by 1 percent and the Japanese stock prices declined by 22 percent on average. However, the same could be said about stocks within a given stock market. Some smaller foreign markets have experienced unusually large gains in some periods. However, it would not be appropriate to conclude that the global stock market environment is inefficient. These same markets also tend to suffer severe declines in some periods.

Capitalizing on Undervalued Foreign Stocks

If U.S. investors believe a particular foreign stock is undervalued, they can attempt to purchase the stock through a brokerage firm. However, the transactions costs are relatively high for foreign stock transactions, and some countries may restrict these transactions. An alternative approach is to purchase the foreign stock on a U.S. stock exchange, if it is listed there. Some of the most well-known foreign stocks are listed on a U.S. stock exchange, but the list is very limited.

An alternative method of investing in undervalued foreign firms is to purchase American depository receipts (ADRs), which are certificates representing ownership of shares of the foreign stock. ADRs can be purchased in the U.S., and therefore do not require foreign stock transactions. They are available for more than 900 foreign firms.

Even when accounting for exchange rate movements, foreign stocks will sometimes generate much higher returns for U.S. investors than U.S.

stocks. However, U.S. investors should recognize that returns on foreign stocks can be very volatile. While there is potential for high return on foreign stocks, there is also a high level of risk. Higher returns on foreign stocks does not necessarily imply market inefficiencies, because of the risk involved. For example, in some less developed countries, stock prices have risen or declined by 90 percent in a single month.

Summary

Markets tend to be less efficient if they are not well developed. Thus, investors searching for undervalued assets may have more success in foreign markets that are not developed. However, the barriers common to less developed markets (such as lack of financial information) may preclude investors from detecting which assets are undervalued.

Discussion

Jordan Company was considering the purchase of a medical supply company in Hungary that was previously state-owned. It was given financial statements by the government on sales and expenses over the last five years. These financial statements showed that sales were stable, and the expenses for wages and equipment were very low. Jordan was attempting to use these statements as possible indicators of the future.

(a) Explain why the historical sales figures may not be accurate indicators of the total future sales.

(b) Explain why the historical expense figures may not be accurate indicators of the total future expenses.

(c) Jordan's executives have stated that the company is severely undervalued. Why would such a company's price not reflect its true value?

14

Multinational Financial Analysis

The interpretation of financial statements by a multinational corporation (MNC) can be extremely difficult because it reflects the consolidation of all subsidiaries. To consolidate subsidiary financial items, the values for each subsidiary must be converted into a common currency. MNCs based in the U.S. have been required to follow Financial Accounting Standards Board (FASB) Statement No. 52 since the early 1980s. The statement requires that income statement items such as revenue, cost of goods sold, depreciation, and other expenses are translated at the weighted average exchange rate over the reporting period of concern. The following discussion explains how the translation can affect the perceived performance of MNCs.

Translation Effects on Earnings

Consider a U.S.-based MNC with one large German subsidiary that had earnings of 100 million deutsche marks (DM) last year, and plans to retain all earnings within Germany. If the German mark had a weighted average exchange rate of $.70 over the reporting period, the earnings would be translated as $70 million. However, if the weighted average exchange rate of the mark was $.60 over the reporting period, the earnings would be translated as $60 million. So for a given amount of actual mark earnings received, there is a difference in reported net income of $10 million between the two scenarios. This example illustrates how the reported consolidated earnings will be reduced whenever the exchange rate used for translation purposes is low. Conversely, the reported consolidated earnings would be high whenever the exchange rate used for translation purposes is high.

Since exchange rates tend to be volatile, they can have a significant impact on an MNC's consolidated earnings in any year. For example, some currencies have recently changed by more than 20 percent in a single year. Those MNCs with a greater proportion of international business will be more exposed to significant translation effects.

Some people may ignore the translation effects, saying that this so-called translation exposure only affects the reported profits on paper, and should have no impact on the MNC's value. Yet, many financial analysts pay very close attention to reported earnings when assessing a firm's financial performance. Thus, the perceived performance is influenced by the exchange rate used for translation.

Hedging Translation Effects on Earnings

If the MNC in our example wishes to hedge translation exposure, it can take a position in a forward contract that offsets its prevailing exposure in a foreign currency. Specifically, it could negotiate a forward contract (with a commercial bank) to sell German marks forward. In the event that the mark depreciates, a given level of mark earnings would be translated into less reported earnings. However, the firm would purchase marks in the spot market just before its forward contract is due and use these marks to fulfill the forward contract. A gain will result from this position, which helps to offset the reduction in reported earnings that resulted from the translation effect.

Limitations of Hedging

Limitations of this strategy to hedge translation effects deserve to be mentioned. Consider the effects if the mark appreciates over the reporting period. The reported consolidated earnings become higher as a result. If a forward hedge was implemented at the beginning of this period to offset translation effects, there would be a loss on the forward position (since the firm would buy marks at a higher exchange rate at the end of the period than what it has agreed to sell marks for to fulfill its forward contract). This loss will offset the translation gain and therefore insulate the reported consolidated earnings from translation effects. However, income ratios such as return on assets will now be understated, because there is still a translation effect on consolidated assets (since assets are translated at the current exchange rate), and no significant translation effect on earnings. Thus, income ratios may not be accurate indicators of performance.

A second limitation of hedging translation effects is that a firm will not necessarily be satisfied when it incurs an actual cash loss from a forward position that is offset by a boost in reported earnings from translation effects. Assuming that the German subsidiary does not remit the earnings, the translation gain is not really realized by the MNC, but is simply a paper gain. Yet, the loss from a forward position is real.

Alternative to Hedging: Communicating to Investors

Given the limitations of hedging translation exposure, some MNCs may prefer not to hedge translation effects on consolidated income. Instead, they may offer an explanation in their financial statements how this consolidated income was distorted by changes in exchange rates. In this way, they may be able to prevent investors from misinterpreting low consolidated earnings that are due mainly to translation effects. The MNCs may even consider highlighting favorable translation effects, so that investors do not use presently overstated consolidated earnings due to translation to create an unusually high expectations of future earnings.

Translation Effects on Financial Ratios

The financial analysis of a firm commonly involves the computation of financial ratios. These ratios can be useful for corporate managers, credit analysts, or investors to evaluate various financial characteristics of the firm. However, there are some limitations associated with the estimation of financial ratios. Most of these limitations (such as multiple industries, variety in accounting practices, and seasonal variation) are summarized in financial management textbooks. However, there is an additional limitation for the financial analysis of any multinational corporations that must be recognized: the distortion of financial ratios due to translation effects. The translation guidelines are described below, along with an explanation of how translation can distort the financial ratios.

Translation Effects of FASB No. 8 on Financial Ratios

In 1975, Financial Accounting Standards Board (FASB) Statement No. 8 was introduced to specify the translation procedure for MNCs. Under FASB Statement No. 8, a foreign subsidiary's inventory and fixed assets were translated at historical exchange rates (when the transactions occurred), while receivables, payables, long-term debt, and other items were translated at current exchange rates. These guidelines led to significant translation effects on the consolidated financial statements of MNCs. For example, if a subsidiary's local currency strengthened against the MNC parent's home currency, the receivables, payables, and long-term debt were translated at high exchange rates while the inventory and fixed assets were translated at low exchange rates. Thus, the debt to assets ratio could be overstated because of the difference in translation effects between balance sheet items. Other financial ratios could also be distorted for the same reasons, and therefore may not be valid indicators of an MNC's financial condition.

Translation Effects of FASB No. 52 on Financial Ratios

In December 1981, FASB Statement No. 52 replaced FASB No. 8, and was adopted by MNCs over the 1981-1983 period. According to FASB Statement No. 52, all balance sheet items except for common equity are translated at the current exchange rate. This adjustment was expected to reduce translation effects because most balance sheet items would be translated at the same exchange rate. However, translation effects could still distort financial ratios when the composition of assets or liabilities at a particular foreign subsidiary deviated from that of the MNC overall.

To illustrate how possible translation effects could distort financial ratios under FASB No. 52, consider a situation where the parent of a U.S.-based multinational corporation with one large foreign subsidiary based in France that functions mainly as a warehouse. Assume the U.S. parent finances the subsidiary by providing long-term loans. The major asset of the warehouse is inventory. When the French franc is strong, the current assets on the consolidated statement are high because of the translation. However, current liabilities would not be subject to translation effects because they are not a major item on the French subsidiary's balance sheet (even though they may be a major item on the parent's balance sheet). Thus, the financial ratios measuring liquidity may not be valid indicators because they may overstate the liquidity. If the French franc was weak, the current assets on the consolidated financial statement would be low because of the translation. Thus, the liquidity ratios could possibly understate the firm's liquidity.

Debt ratios would also be subject to translation effects because of the long-term debt carried on the subsidiary's balance sheet. When the franc is strong, the debt is translated at a high exchange rate, which may cause the debt ratios to overstate the firm's degree of financial leverage. When the franc is weak, the debt ratios understate the firm's degree of financial leverage. Income ratios can be distorted because of the translation effects on earnings (as described earlier).

Summary

The financial condition of any MNCs with foreign subsidiaries can be distorted by translation effects. The potential distortion has been reduced with the adoption of FASB Statement No. 52. However, translation can still distort reported earnings and various financial ratios, especially when the balance sheet composition at subsidiaries is much different than the overall composition of the MNC. The assessment of an MNC's financial condition can still be enhanced with the estimation of financial ratios, but any possible bias resulting from translation effects should be recognized.

Discussion

Jordan's financial analysts were assessing its consolidated financial statements to determine its degree of financial leverage. Its foreign subsidiaries used long–term debt as their main source of funds. The U.S. parent used mostly equity as its main source of funds. The dollar was unusually strong against most currencies in the recent year relative to most years. The analysts found that the debt/equity ratio from the consolidated balance sheet was high, but within the upper end of the range for the industry. Most other firms in the industry have virtually all of their operations in the U.S. The analysts concluded that the financial leverage of Jordan was acceptable.

(a) Do you agree with the conclusion of the financial analysts? Explain.

(b) Jordan's financial leverage as measured by debt/equity is lower this year than in previous years. Is there any reason to believe that this result is misleading?

15

Multinational Financial Planning

Corporate managers must attempt to anticipate changes in economic conditions when they conduct financial planning. For example, the feasibility of a firm expanding some of its businesses will be dependent on expected future cash flows, which are influenced by the strength of the economy. Decisions about the amount of cash and inventory to maintain are influenced by forecasted sales, which are affected by economic conditions.

To the extent that foreign economies influence local economic conditions, they can affect a firm's policies. Therefore, corporate managers must monitor foreign economies to anticipate possible changes in the local economy. The global impact can be on the entire domestic economy or on the particular industry of the firm.

Global Impact on the U.S. Economy

The strength of an economy is influenced by the aggregate demand for goods and services in that economy. The aggregate demand can be affected by foreign conditions. A portion of the aggregate demand is foreign demand for goods and services in the domestic economy.

One factor that affects foreign demand is the strength of the foreign economies. If national incomes are growing in foreign countries, foreign demand for U.S. products will increase, and therefore cause U.S. economic growth to increase.

A second factor that can affect foreign demand is the value of the dollar. If the dollar weakens, foreign customers pay less for U.S. goods, and therefore will increase their demand for U.S. goods. A weak dollar can also make foreign goods expensive from the U.S. perspective, and therefore increase the demand by U.S. households and firms for U.S. products. A stronger dollar has the opposite effect.

The aggregate demand for goods and services in a domestic economy can also be highly influenced by domestic interest rates. To the extent that global conditions affect domestic interest rates, they can affect domestic economy, and therefore have an indirect influence on domestic firms. To illustrate, consider that the interest rates are dictated by the interaction of demand for funds and supply of funds available. As foreign investors deposit funds in the U.S., the supply of available funds rises, and there is downward pressure on U.S. interest rates. A decline in interest rates can influence the amount of spending because households and firms are more willing to borrow.

Conversely, the withdrawal of funds by foreign investors from the U.S. reduces the supply of available funds, and places upward pressure on U.S. interest rates. The performance of many firms will be affected by the shift in interest rates. For example, domestic sales by automobile manufacturers are closely linked with domestic interest rates, since the demand for automobiles is partially determined by the financing rate. If foreign investors withdrew funds from the U.S., interest rates would rise, the financing rate on automobiles would rise, and the demand for automobiles would decline.

Effects of Global Economic Conditions

While the global conditions can influence the domestic firms indirectly through their impact on the domestic economy, they can even have a more direct effect on some U.S. firms. The effects on U.S. exporting firms, U.S. importing firms, and foreign subsidiaries of U.S.-based multinational corporations (MNCs) are discussed below.

Effects on U.S. Exporting Firms

Consider a U.S. firm that generates 30 percent of its sales from exporting to European countries. The European demand for this firm's product will be directly affected by the national incomes in European currencies. All U.S. exporting firms should be directly affected by global conditions.

Effects on U.S. Importing Firms

Consider a U.S. firm that purchases most of its materials (denominated in British pounds) from a British firm. The price paid for these materials will be increased if the British firm increases its prices or if the pound appreciates against the dollar. Any economic conditions in the United Kingdom (such as inflation) that could either affect that British firm's pricing policy or the value of the pound will affect the U.S. firm's cost of materials, and therefore affect its earnings.

Effects on Subsidiaries of U.S.-Based MNCs

Consider a U.S. firm with foreign subsidiaries in other countries. If the subsidiaries were established to produce products for sale in those foreign countries, the firm's performance is directly influenced by the economic conditions of those countries. Large automobile manufacturers with plants and dealerships overseas closely monitor the national incomes in the foreign countries when determining their production levels. They also monitor foreign interest rates, since the demand for automobiles in these foreign countries is influenced by consumer financing rates.

Inflation in the foreign countries can affect labor costs, costs of machinery, and leasing costs at foreign subsidiaries. The changing costs may affect decisions on capital expenditures, and may also influence the earnings of the foreign subsidiaries.

Effects of Foreign Competition

Global conditions can also affect firms through specific industry effects. For example, foreign competitors in particular industries may invest heavily in research and development, to improve technology. These global industry conditions may modify financial decisions by the domestic producers in that industry, such as research and development expenditures necessary to remain competitive.

Foreign competition can intensify over time in various industries as a result of reductions in the cost of financing. For example, when interest rates are lower in Japan than the U.S., the cost of financing by Japanese firms is less than the cost of financing by U.S. firms. Thus, Japanese firms could possibly charge lower prices and still maintain an adequate level of earnings, because their financing costs are lower.

As a related example, consider a U.S. firm with no foreign sales, but assume that its main competitor is based in Canada and exports its products (denominated in the Canadian dollar) to the U.S. If the Canadian dollar weakens against the U.S. dollar, U.S. consumers may switch to the Canadian firm because they will now pay less dollars for that firm's product. Thus, the U.S. firm with no foreign business is directly affected by changes in the value of the dollar.

Effects of Trade Barriers

Trade barriers represent another type of global effect on particular industries. For example, the sales forecasts of U.S. automobile producers may be increased by quotas imposed on foreign automobiles exported to the U.S. Thus, the U.S. firm's financial policies on capital expenditures, amount of financing needed, and amount of inventory to maintain would be affected as well. If the automobile producers did not account for quotas, they may underestimate future sales, and therefore underestimate the amount of capital expenditures, the amount of financing, and the amount of inventory needed to support future sales.

Since trade barriers vary across industries, they affect the financial policies of firms in different ways. In some industries, there are no barriers on goods exported to the U.S., but there are barriers on goods exported by the U.S. The U.S. exporting firms in these industries must attempt to forecast how such barriers will limit their export sales, so that they can determine the proper amount of financing needed for future growth, and the optimal inventory of finished goods to maintain.

As trade barriers are imposed, firms search for ways to circumvent them. Thus, trade barriers will not necessarily reduce foreign competition. As an example, if quotas are imposed on foreign automobiles exported to the U.S., some foreign automobile manufacturers may establish subsidiaries in the U.S. to produce the automobiles locally. U.S. firms must consider such a possibility when assessing whether their sales will increase in response to quotas on foreign imports.

Effects of Foreign Political Conditions

Political conditions in foreign countries can also affect financial policies of U.S. firms. For example, the political reform in Eastern Europe encourages financial managers of U.S. firms to assess the feasibility of exporting or establishing subsidiaries there. Such polices were not even considered prior to the reform. Adverse political conditions, such as excessive taxation imposed on foreign subsidiaries, may force U.S. firms to sell these subsidiaries.

Summary

U.S. firms commonly conduct their financial planning by assessing the economic and political climate and industry conditions. Any U.S. firm that has any international business or competes with foreign firms must conduct their analysis with a global perspective. Global conditions can affect demand for the U.S. firm's products, pricing, all types of expenses, and even taxes. Every item on a firm's income statement may be affected by economic conditions, political conditions, and industry conditions (such as competition) in foreign countries. U.S. firms that are more globally aware of the global conditions make more informed financial decisions.

Discussion

Based on the common international business transactions of Jordan Co. as illustrated in Figure 15.1, perform the following tasks.

   (a) Given Jordan's existing international business, describe some specific types of global conditions that will affect its overall performance.

Figure 15.1
Illustration of Jordan's International Business

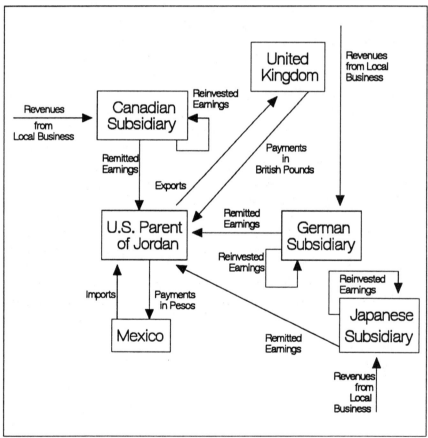

(b) Explain how specific types of global conditions could affect the level of sales by Jordan's parent.

16

Multinational Cash Budgeting

Two key factors that influence the forecasted cash at the end of every period are sales and purchases. For firms involved in international business, the forecast of each factor is dependent on international conditions. First, the cash budget for a U.S. firm engaging in international trade transactions is discussed, followed by a discussion of the budget for a U.S. firm with foreign subsidiaries

Cash Budgeting for Firms Conducting International Trade

The discussion of cash budgeting by firms that conduct international trade focuses on the impact of exporting, followed by the impact of importing.

Impact of Exporting on the Cash Budget

For U.S. firms that derive some of their sales from exports to foreign countries, the forecast of sales is partially dependent on the economies of those countries. Demand for U.S. exports is normally expected to increase when economic growth rises in foreign countries. The magnitude of the increased demand varies with the type of product sold, as the demand for some products are less sensitive to economic conditions.

A second international condition affecting forecasted sales is the status of trade barriers. If foreign governments are expected to place a tariff or quota on products exported by the U.S. firm, forecasted sales must be reduced accordingly. Unfortunately, it is sometimes difficult to anticipate such a government policy, especially for some developing countries.

International sales can also be affected by foreign inflation rates, since higher local prices in the foreign countries relative to the U.S. may result in an increased demand for U.S. exports. The U.S. firm will especially experience an increased market share if most competitors are in those foreign countries.

Sales can also be affected by exchange rate movements. When foreign currencies appreciate against the dollar, foreign demand for U.S. exports should increase. The magnitude of the increase varies not only with the degree of appreciation, but also with the characteristics of competitive firms. If the competition is in the U.S., none of the firms gain a competitive advantage, although they may all benefit from increased aggregate demand for the product. If the competition is mostly in foreign countries, appreciation of the foreign currencies will typically cause an increase in sales for the U.S. firm. However, some foreign competitors may reduce their price to maintain their market share. If foreign currencies depreciate against the dollar, foreign demand for a U.S. firm's exports would typically decline, especially if there are some foreign competitors that serve the foreign markets and are not affected by the currency movements.

It is sometimes suggested that inflation differential between countries can be offset by exchange rate adjustments, as stated by the purchasing power parity (PPP) theory. In this case, the currency of a country with high inflation would weaken, so that the demand for a U.S. firm's goods would not be substantially affected. However, there is very clear evidence that because exchange rate movements respond to other factors in addition to inflation, an offsetting effect is unlikely, especially in the short run.

Impact of Importing on the Cash Budget

U.S. firms that make some foreign purchases of supplies and materials must consider the possibility of U.S. quotas or tariffs on their imports, which could affect their cash outflows. In addition, inflation in the U.S. can cause an increase in their purchases overseas, which increase the amount of foreign currency needed. Any appreciation of the foreign currencies they need will increase their cash outflows for purchases, unless they could switch to a local competitor. Conversely, depreciation of the currencies needed would reduce their cash outflows.

Overall, the forecast of sales will be positively related to the economies of the importing countries and the degree of appreciation in foreign currencies of these countries. The forecast of purchases will be positively related to the degree of depreciation in foreign currencies needed by the U.S. firm. The general effects of exporting and importing on a U.S. firm's cash budget are illustrated in Figure 16.1. The effects should be more pronounced for firms that have a larger proportion of foreign sales relative to their total sales.

Cash Budgeting for MNCs with Foreign Subsidiaries

For a multinational corporation (MNC) with foreign subsidiaries, the cash budgeting procedure can be overwhelming. The first step is to consider each subsidiary as a separate entity, so that a cash budget is created for each. This allows the MNC to estimate the amount of excess or deficient cash for each subsidiary in each month. While the cash budgeting could be conducted by the parent for each separate subsidiary, it will require substantial input from each subsidiary to derive forecasted cash inflows and outflows per month. For example, information will be needed from each subsidiary on sales, accounts receivable collections, purchases, wages, rent, and taxes. The parent could assign managers at each subsidiary to develop their own cash budget, but should participate in the process to assure that each subsidiary uses similar guidelines. If each cash budget is conducted using different guidelines, the budgets could not be compared or consolidated in any manner.

Figure 16.1
International Effects on Cash Budgeting

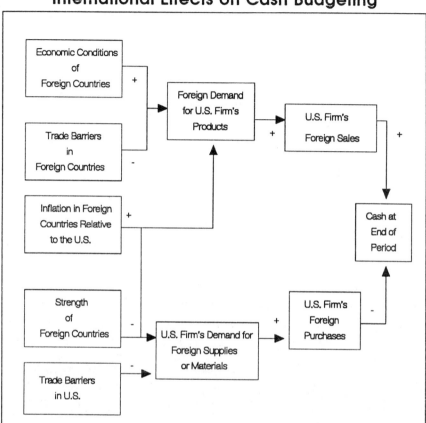

The completion of cash budgets for all subsidiaries is only the first step. The next step is to interpret the implications of each cash budget. That is, will the subsidiary typically have excess cash, or will it experience cash shortages in upcoming months? If it has excess cash, where should the cash be invested? If it will experience cash shortages, how should it obtain funds to cover the cash deficiency?

It is common for MNCs to use inter-subsidiary cash transfers from subsidiaries with excess cash to those with cash shortages. To facilitate this process, the surplus or deficient cash balance for each subsidiary in each month should be measured, and then translated to a U.S. dollar value so that this balance can be compared among subsidiaries. Then, the MNC can address the questions on how to handle each subsidiary's expected cash surplus or deficiency.

Example

To illustrate, consider the cash balance for each of four subsidiaries of a U.S.-based MNC over the next three months:

Expected Surplus (or Deficit) Cash
Balance in Millions of Units (– implies deficit)

Subsidiary based in	January	February	March
Canada	C$30	C$20	-C$30
France	FF50	-FF30	FF20
Germany	-DM10	-DM5	-DM20
Switzerland	SF20	SF30	-SF10

Given the firm's forecast of the mean exchange rate of each currency with respect to the dollar during this three-month period shown in the second column of the following table, the translated dollar value of the surplus or deficit is shown:

Translated Expected Surplus (or Deficit) Cash Balance (in millions of $)

Subsidiary based in	Forecasted Exchange Rate	January	February	March
Canada	C$=$.80	$24	$16	-$24
France	FF=$.20	$10	-$6	$4
Germany	DM=$.60	-$6	-$3	-$12
Switzerland	SF=$.70	$14	$21	-$7

If exchange rates were forecasted per month, more precise estimates of the dollar value of the cash balance or surplus per subsidiary could possibly be derived in each month. It should be emphasized that the cash surplus or deficiency is simply translated to dollars to compare the magnitudes using a common denominator. From this table, it is clear that the cash shortage experienced by the German subsidiary in January could be covered by transferring excess cash from any of the other three foreign subsidiaries. In February, the combined cash shortages of the French and German subsidiaries could be covered by transferring excess cash from either of the other foreign subsidiaries. The actual decision on whether funds should be borrowed from a local bank or another subsidiary, or which subsidiary should provide the loan is dependent on additional factors such as interest rates in the host countries of the subsidiaries.

In March, three of the foreign subsidiaries are expected to experience a cash shortage, which cannot be covered by the French subsidiary. Thus, the subsidiaries will need to obtain funds elsewhere, perhaps from local banks. The cash budget has signaled that these subsidiaries should assure that they can obtain loans from local banks in March.

To determine whether the subsidiaries should plan to borrow funds for just a few months or for a longer period, the cash balances should be estimated for each subsidiary over several months. If one or more foreign subsidiaries is expected to experience a consistent cash shortage over several months that cannot be covered by the other subsidiaries, a loan of one year or longer may be necessary.

Cash budgeting of an MNC with foreign subsidiaries is like a portfolio of cash budgets for individual subsidiaries, translated to a single currency. Proper cash budgeting by MNCs assures the most efficient use of cash and warns the MNC of any possible liquidity problems in the future. The estimated cash surplus or deficiency per subsidiary cannot be measured by accounting statements since cash inflows and outflows can lag reports of revenue and expenses.

Summary

Forecasts of international conditions are necessary to forecast a U.S. firm's sales and purchases, which are then used to estimate a cash budget. Since the forecasts of international conditions are uncertain, so are the forecasts of international purchases and sales. However, the firm's cash budget would typically be even less accurate if the international conditions were not considered.

Discussion

The Treasurer of Jordan Company had recently constructed the cash budget for the U.S. parent, which includes not only its U.S. business but also its cash flows resulting from importing and exporting, as well as cash inflows resulting from earnings remitted by foreign subsidiaries. Today, Jordan's financial analysts and economists revised economic forecasts. Jordan's international transactions are shown in Figure 16.2, which can be reviewed when answering the following questions.

(a) Explain how the forecasted cash balance of the U.S. parent will be influenced by a substantial upward revision of Mexican inflation (assume the peso's forecasted value is not affected).

(b) Explain how the forecasted cash balance of the U.S. parent will be influenced by a substantial downward revision of the dollar's forecasted strength relative to all currencies except the peso.

(c) Explain how the forecasted cash balance of the U.S. parent will be affected by increased corporate taxes in Germany and Japan.

Figure 16.2
Illustration of Jordan's International Business

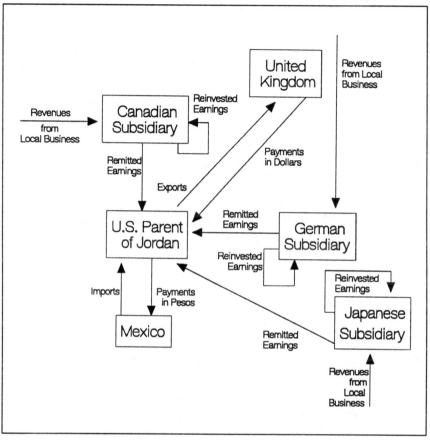

17

Multinational Cash Management

Cash management of a multinational corporation (MNC) is more complex than that of a purely domestic firm. Consider an MNC as a combination of subsidiaries across various countries. Each subsidiary must maintain adequate liquidity in case of temporary deficiencies in net cash flows. Thus, an MNC's cash management essentially requires the monitoring of several separate entities.

Centralized Cash Management

A centralized system can make an MNC's cash management more efficient. First, a centralized system can monitor all subsidiary transactions and determine the net amount that one subsidiary owes the other at the end of each month. For example, the Canadian and German subsidiaries may be assessed daily charges as a result of ordering materials from each other. In this case, only one net payment is made per month. Thus, the transactions costs associated with the conversion of one currency to another are minimized.

A centralized system can also monitor the cash balances of each subsidiary, so that it may request the transfer of funds from subsidiaries with excess cash to subsidiaries with deficient cash. With this system, subsidiaries do not need to hold large amounts of cash, as they can borrow from other subsidiaries if they experience a cash deficiency. Such a system reduces the need for outside funding and can reduce interest expenses for the overall MNC.

Risk–Return Tradeoff

A key Treasury decision of an MNC's cash management is where to invest the cash. Each subsidiary could simply purchase Treasury bills or other high quality money market securities in its respective country. Alternatively, each subsidiary may consider investing in the money market securities of foreign countries. Interest rate differentials of 6 percentage points or more are common across industrialized countries, which may encourage the subsidiary in a country with low interest rates to invest the cash elsewhere. This involves conversion to a different currency before investing in a country with high interest rates, thereby exposing the subsidiary to exchange rate risk. There is a risk–return tradeoff to consider. The subsidiary will normally be exposed to exchange rate risk if it invests in securities denominated in a foreign country, unless it will need that foreign currency (to purchase supplies, etc.) at a future point in time.

Hedging the Exchange Rate Risk

If the subsidiary invests cash in a foreign currency with a relatively high interest rate and has no future need for that currency, it will reconvert back to its local currency at a future point in time. It could hedge the exchange rate risk by negotiating a forward contract with a commercial bank, in which it agrees to exchange the currency back to its local currency at a specified exchange rate (called the forward rate) at a specified future point in time. However, the so-called forward rate at which the funds will be reconverted will contain a discount relative to the spot (or current) exchange rate, which will typically offset any interest rate advantage. This relationship between the interest rate differential of two countries and the forward rate is known as interest rate parity.

For example, if a U.S. subsidiary attempts to invest its excess cash in France for one year because the interest rate is 3 percentage points higher there, the forward rate on the French franc would contain a discount of about 3 percent. This discount offsets the 3 percent interest rate advantage, so that investing in a country with higher interest rates is not superior to investing in the home country.

Remaining Exposed to Exchange Rate Risk

Because of the offsetting effect described above, subsidiaries would not normally hedge their foreign money market investments with forward contracts. Therefore, the subsidiaries will be exposed to exchange rate risk, but may still be willing to invest in foreign money market securities if the expected returns on investments are high enough.

The expected return can be written as:

$$r = (1 + i) \times (1 + e) - 1$$

where i represents the interest rate on the foreign money market securities and e represents the expected percentage change in the currency denominating the currency. While the interest rate on the money market securities is known, the exchange rate percentage change is not. The return to a firm from a foreign investment in money market securities will be higher than investing in local money market securities as long as the exchange rate effect does not offset the interest rate advantage.

For example, consider a U.S. subsidiary that could either invest in French money market securities for one year at 11 percent or U.S. money market securities at 8 percent. Assume that it expects the franc to depreciate against the dollar by 2 percent over this period. The expected return to the U.S. subsidiary if it invests in French money market securities for one year is:

$$
\begin{aligned}
r &= (1 + i) \times (1 + e) - 1 \\
&= (1 + .11) \times [1 + (-.02)] - 1 \\
&= .0878 \text{ or } 8.78\%
\end{aligned}
$$

Thus, the subsidiary may choose to invest its funds in the franc, but must keep in mind that if its forecast of e is incorrect, so will be its forecast of r. For example, if the franc depreciates by 6 percent instead of 2 percent, the return from investing in the French money market securities would be:

$$r = (1 + i) \times (1 + e) - 1$$
$$= (1 + .11) \times [1 + (-.06)] - 1$$
$$= .0434 \text{ or } 4.34\%$$

which is less than the 8 percent return on local securities. This illustrates how investment of excess cash in foreign money market securities with high interest rates can sometimes backfire. A subsidiary is more likely to invest cash in foreign securities if it is confident that the currency denominating those securities will not depreciate against its local currency.

The return from investing in foreign money market securities could be enhanced if the foreign currency appreciates against the subsidiary's local currency. Using our previous example, if the franc appreciated by 7 percent against the dollar, the return from investing in French money market securities would be:

$$r = (1 + i) \times (1 + e) - 1$$
$$= (1 + .11) \times (1.07) - 1$$
$$= 18.77\%$$

But the firm must realize that while there is potential for higher return, there is also uncertainty about the return resulting from exchange rate risk. The higher the probability that the franc could depreciate over the investment period, the higher is the probability that the foreign investment could backfire.

Reducing Risk through Diversification

When U.S. firms invest in foreign money market securities, they assess two types of risk: default risk and exchange rate risk. To reduce default risk, they tend to focus on either securities issued by the national governments, or securities issued by large corporations with low risk. They may also attempt to diversify their foreign investments across countries so that they are somewhat insulated if poor economic conditions raise the level of default risk on securities issued in any particular country.

U.S. firms are also concerned with exchange rate risk. The high degree of exchange rate volatility has caused the effective (exchange rate-adjusted) yields on foreign money market securities to be volatile. Some U.S. firms attempt to stabilize the returns on their foreign money market investments though international diversification. In this way, the U.S. firm reduces its exposure to any individual foreign currency. The degree to which the diversification across currencies can reduce exchange rate risk is dependent on how correlated the movements of these currencies are against the dollar. If the currency movements against the dollar are highly correlated, diversification will not be very effective. All individual foreign currencies could possibly decline simultaneously against the dollar, thereby adversely affecting the yields of all of the firm's foreign money market investments. Since exchange rates of European currencies have historically moved in tandem against the dollar, diversification by U.S. firms across European currencies may not significantly reduce the firm's exposure to exchange rate risk. A more viable approach would be diversification across continents, so that the foreign investments are denominated in currencies whose movements against the dollar are not highly correlated.

Effective Yields on Foreign Money Market Investments

The effective yields generated by U.S. firms from investing in foreign currencies of most industrialized countries were very high in the late 1980s, because these currencies strengthened against the dollar. However, the effective yields were very low and sometimes even negative in the early 1990s because these foreign currencies weakened against the dollar. A negative effective yield implies that when the foreign money market investment matures, the principal and interest convert to a smaller amount of funds than the firm initially invested. This occurs only when the depreciation in the foreign currency overwhelms the interest rate earned on the investment.

Using the Forward Rate to Forecast Effective Yields

Since exchange rates are difficult to forecast, so are the effective yields on investments in foreign money market instruments. The U.S. firm may use the corresponding forward rate as a forecast for the future spot rate of the currency, and then derive the expected percentage change in the exchange rate to determine a forecast for the effective yield. However, recall that under conditions of interest rate parity, the forward rate will reflect the differential between the two interest rates. Therefore, the forecasted effective yield of the foreign investment when using the forward rate to forecast the spot exchange rate at maturity will be equal to a yield that the U.S. firm could earn in the U.S. Thus, the only way that the U.S. firm would expect to earn a higher rate of return on the foreign investment is if its forecast for the future spot rate exceeds the forward rate.

Summary

International cash management involves optimum use of any excess cash. U.S.-based MNCs transfer cash among subsidiaries to assure that cash is being put to its best use. When an MNC has excess cash that is not needed by any of its subsidiaries, it attempts to earn a reasonable return while maintaining risk at a tolerable level. It may consider investing the funds in those foreign money market securities where interest rates are high. However, it must forecast the respective exchange rate movements against the dollar to forecast the effective yield. It can then measure the potential extra yield (if any) on the foreign investment to determine whether foreign investment is worth the risk.

Discussion

The parent of Jordan Co. has excess funds which it can use to invest for one year. It could invest in German marks at 10 percent, in U.S. dollars at 9 percent, or in Mexican pesos at 32 percent. The German mark is expected to depreciate by 1 percent against the dollar, while the Mexican peso is expected to depreciate by 20 percent against the dollar. Jordan's three investment choices are displayed in Figure 17.1.

(a) What is the expected effective yield on the investment in marks? In pesos?

(b) Where should Jordan invest its funds?

(c) Is there a way in which Jordan can take advantage of the high Mexican interest rate, while using its existing business transactions to cover the exchange rate risk?

Figure 17.1
Short–Term Investment Alternatives

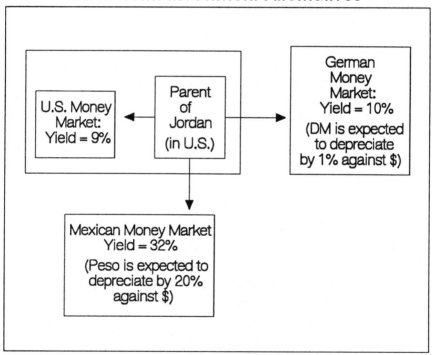

18

Credit Policies of Multinational Corporations

Most firms have a credit policy that provides a set of guidelines on the credit granted to customers. A proper credit policy is especially relevant for any exporting conducted by firms. Some of the key elements of a credit policy are discussed below, with an emphasis on how they relate to exporting.

Elements of Credit Policy

Three key elements of credit policy are:

(1) The credit granting decision (who receives credit?).

(2) The credit period allowed for customers to make their payment.

(3) The means of assuring that customers will repay the credit they are granted.

The first element determines the allocation of credit to customers that appear to be creditworthy. The second element reflects the timing of the cash inflows to be received from selling products. Firms prefer to expedite the cash inflows because they can then use that cash to meet payment obligations or to make investments. The third element reflects the assurance that the future cash flows resulting from credit granted will arrive as anticipated.

Problems with Global Credit

The granting of credit on exports is a concern for the following reasons. First, the transportation time involved in exporting goods can stretch the so-called working capital cycle from when costs of production were incurred until the payment is received. When the payment is not sent until goods are received, the transportation time causes a further delay in the receipt of cash. There is also an additional delay because of the time taken for the check from the foreign customers to arrive and clear.

To resolve the problem of a delay in receiving payment because of transportation time, the exporting firm may request that foreign customers make payment immediately. That is, the longer transportation time is offset by a shorter period between customer receipt of goods and payment. However, this policy could encourage some foreign customers to purchase their goods elsewhere. The exporting firm may entice the foreign customers by offering a discount if quick payment is made. Of course, the benefits from receiving the payment earlier may be offset by the reduction in payment received.

When U.S. exporting firms accept foreign currency as payment, the cost of a delay in payment may vary with the currency, for two possible reasons. First, each currency has its own interest rate, so that the opportunity cost from a delayed payment could be measured as the foregone interest earned if the currency could have been invested. Second, each currency has its own exchange rate against the dollar, so that a delay in payments of weakening currencies could result in less dollars. U.S. exporting firms would incur a higher cost of delay for currencies that are expected to weaken over time. Thus, they may be more willing to allow a discount for immediate payment when the currency to be received is likely to weaken.

A second problem is that the exporting firms may be uncomfortable granting credit to firms in other countries, because of the difficulty in assessing credit of foreign customers, and collecting payment from foreign customers who do not pay. Solutions to this concern about global credit risk follow.

Protection Against Global Credit Risk

Some possible solutions regarding the problem of being unable to efficiently evaluate creditworthiness of foreign customers and assuring that they make their payments include:

- request payment before sending goods,
- use letters of credit,
- use agencies that provide protection,
- sell the accounts receivable to factors.

These solutions are discussed below.

Request Payment before Sending Goods

An exporter can avoid global credit risk by requesting that the importer pay for the exported goods before they are sent. The exporter could then send the goods after making sure the check clears. However, some importers may be unwilling to send a check until they receive the goods. In addition, they may need the goods immediately.

Use Letters of Credit

A second possible solution is to use a letter of credit. A letter of credit is issued by a commercial bank on behalf of the foreign customer (importer) promising to make payment to the exporter once the shipping documents are received. Thus, as long as the bank can be trusted to fulfill its promise, the exporting firm does not need to evaluate the credit-worthiness of the foreign customers. While this strategy is effective, there is a cost. Banks will charge a fee to issue a letter of credit. In essence, the exporting firm pays a fee to a bank to insulate itself from the possibility of nonpayment by foreign firms.

Use Agencies that Provide Protection

Some agencies such as the Export–Import Bank called ("Eximbank") have been established to alleviate problems associated with global credit risk. Eximbank will sometimes help finance the manufacture of goods that will ultimately be exported. This reduces any cash flow problems to exporting firms that could result from late payment. The Eximbank can also provide protection against risk of nonpayment by foreign customers due to political risk (such as a change in government regimes that prevents the foreign customers from making payment). This reduces the risk from the granting of credit to foreign customers. However, some degree of credit risk to the exporting firm still exists because foreign customers may not pay for other reasons (such as going bankrupt just after receiving the goods).

Sell the Accounts Receivable to Factors

Another possible solution to credit assessment problems is factoring. The exporter can sell its accounts receivable to a so-called factor, that specializes in collecting the receivables. Factors purchase accounts receivable from firms at a discount, usually on a nonrecourse basis (which means the factor bears the loss if the receivables are not paid).

When exporters sell receivables to factors, they receive cash at that time from the factor, thereby avoiding any further delay in payment. In addition, they no longer need to worry about the creditworthiness of the importers. However, the cost to the exporters is the discount on the sale of the receivables. The magnitude of the discount paid by the factor for the receivables should reflect the perceived creditworthiness of the importer. Thus, the cost to exporters is positively related to the risk that the receivables will not be paid. Factors are more able to collect on receivables because it is their specialty, and they may have subsidiaries in foreign countries that facilitate the collection process.

Credit Policies for Transactions Between Subsidiaries

An MNC may establish a credit policy for its subsidiaries that sell goods to each other. This policy may be more lenient than the policy for sales to unrelated customers, because it can be assured that its subsidiaries will act in good faith. Nevertheless, the policy may still specify a maximum period in which credit can be offered by one subsidiary. If credit is granted for excessive periods, the importing subsidiary benefits at the expense of the exporting subsidiary, because it has use of the funds until the payment is made. To the extent that the subsidiaries are evaluated based on performance, any transactions between subsidiaries should be conducted as if they are unrelated. Yet, the MNC can typically avoid letters of credit or factoring for transactions between subsidiaries.

Summary

Exporting firms must deal with two specific problems related to credit policy: (1) a delay in payments received, and (2) inability to properly evaluate creditworthiness of foreign customers or to force payment. While there are ways to deal with these problems, there is a cost involved. Exporting may still be feasible, but such costs should be recognized when considering whether to export. An effective global credit policy can maintain any cash delays or credit risks to a tolerable level, and may therefore encourage firms to export.

Discussion

Jordan Co. periodically exports goods to the United Kingdom. Its customers include (1) hospitals owned by the government that order supplies on monthly basis, and (2) other privately owned medical firms that normally purchase supplies from other sources, but order supplies from the parent on an infrequent basis.

(a) What type of credit policy might be used for the hospitals owned by the government?

(b) What type of credit policy might be used for the privately owned medical firms?

19

Inventory Management of Multinational Corporations

Inventory management requires policies for how much inventory to maintain, and where to maintain it. Since these policies are influenced by characteristics of the firm, the inventory policies of multinational corporations (MNCs) may differ from those of domestic corporations. The characteristics of MNCs that affect inventory policies are discussed here.

Factors Affecting the Amount of Inventory Held by MNCs

The amount of inventory to maintain is partially influenced by the anticipated demand for products and the speed at which inventory can be replenished. If demand is somewhat stable over time, less inventory is needed because the risk of running short (stockouts) is lower. However, if demand is erratic, the firm may hold a large inventory to avoid the possibility of stockouts. Global conditions can affect the anticipated demand for products and the speed at which inventory can be replenished, and can therefore affect the optimal level of inventory. Some of the more obvious global conditions that must be considered by MNCs when managing inventories are:

- economic growth in foreign countries,
- exchange rate movements,
- global production process,
- trade barriers.

Each of these characteristics is discussed below.

Economic Growth in Foreign Countries

An MNC must consider the sources of demand for its products. For example, if most of the demand comes from Canada, France, and Germany, the MNC must assess the future economic growth of these countries so that it can estimate the demand for its products, and therefore the optimal inventories to maintain. When MNCs expect higher economic growth in foreign countries, they normally forecast an increase in sales and therefore boost inventories. Of course, the demand for some goods may be more responsive to a change in economic growth than others.

Exchange Rate Movements

The demand for some products sold by MNCs can be more erratic because of exchange rate risk. For example, consider a U.S. firm that exports goods denominated in dollars to the United Kingdom. If the British pound appreciates by 10 percent against the dollar, British customers can purchase 10 percent more of the exports without spending any more than before. Thus, exporting firms may wish to maintain more inventory in the event that exchange rates shift. Conversely, if the pound depreciates, the British demand for the U.S. firm's exports will be reduced if there are firms in the United Kingdom that sell similar goods.

In some cases in which the U.S. dollar denominating the exports appears to be very weak and likely to strengthen, foreign customers may demand large amounts immediately to take advantage of the relatively low price (from their perspective). In this case, U.S. exporting firms would need to maintain relatively large inventories to prepare for a possible increase in the foreign demand. If the firm does not have adequate inventory to accommodate the foreign demand, the foreign customers may shift to a competing U.S. firm that sells the same product. The customers may even decide to switch permanently to the competing firm. Such possible adverse effects may encourage firms to maintain large inventories to prepare for erratic shifts in demand caused by exchange rate fluctuations.

Global Production Process

Another factor that can influence inventories of MNCs is the global production process at foreign subsidiaries. Consider a situation in which some parts needed to assemble the product are produced at foreign subsidiaries and shipped to the U.S. plant. If the plant runs out of these parts, there will be longer delays because of the relatively long time needed to transport the parts (unless the parts are small enough that they can be sent through express mail). To avoid any long delays, firms that rely on parts from foreign subsidiaries may maintain a larger inventory.

Consider an alternative situation in which firms rely on unrelated foreign suppliers for parts. The possibility of delivery delays may be even greater because they have no control over the production schedule of the foreign suppliers. Thus, they should maintain higher inventories.

Trade Barriers

MNCs must also consider trade barriers when managing inventories. If the MNC uses supplies produced in foreign countries, it may maintain larger inventories for those supplies that could be subject to future trade barriers. This would give them more time to search for an alternative source of supplies before they experience stockouts.

Some countries are much more likely to enact trade barriers than others. In addition, some industries may be more prone to trade barriers because of lobbying power of special interest groups. Firms could assess the likelihood of trade barriers and the difficulty in switching to an alternative supplier when deciding whether a larger inventory is necessary.

Cost of Maintaining Inventories

While maintaining a higher inventory reduces the risk of stockouts, it can be costly. Higher inventory levels require a higher investment, which ties up more funds that could have been used for other purposes. Since these funds could have been invested in marketable securities instead of additional inventory, the firm is incurring an opportunity cost. This cost is higher when interest rates on securities are higher. The opportunity cost associated with maintaining additional inventory at a given point in time varies among countries because interest rates vary among countries. For example, the opportunity cost will typically be relatively high in countries such as Australia and Italy, where interest rates are usually higher. Conversely, the opportunity cost will be lower in countries such as Japan and Switzerland, where interest rates are usually lower. Thus, even if all other operating characteristics were similar, one subsidiary may be willing to hold more inventory than another because its opportunity costs are lower.

The Inventory Location Decision

Another inventory decision for MNCs is where to maintain the inventory? Consider an MNC that produces a product in the U.S., but distributes the product worldwide. Should the MNC maintain the inventory in the U.S. or at each of the foreign subsidiaries where the products are distributed? The advantage of maintaining the inventory at each foreign subsidiary is that the costs of continually sending just enough inventory to the subsidiary could be prohibitive. It is normally more efficient to send inventory in bulk, to reduce reorder frequency and transportation costs. However, if all subsidiaries have their own inventories, the overall inventory level will typically be large, which could reflect a high opportunity cost.

Centralization of Inventories

If inventory could have been maintained at some central location and sent upon demand by subsidiaries, less inventory would be maintained in aggregate. Even if a few foreign subsidiaries needed more inventory than expected at a given period, others may not need as much inventory as expected. Thus, by maintaining all inventories in one place, numerous subsidiaries would not be holding excessive inventories. Conversely, when each foreign subsidiary maintains its own additional inventory to prepare for a possible increase in demand, many of these excess inventories will not be used.

One obvious limitation with maintaining the inventories at one central location is the delay in transferring the inventories to any foreign subsidiaries that need them. Because of this limitation, each foreign subsidiary may prefer to maintain some level of inventories so that it avoids stockouts while waiting for orders to be transported from a central location.

Transferring Inventories Across Subsidiaries

Ideally, an MNC would like to have a system in which subsidiaries with surplus inventories can help out other subsidiaries that are short of inventories. All subsidiaries of an MNC could maintain less inventories if they could rely on those of other subsidiaries. However, if the subsidiaries are not close to each other, the costs of continually transferring inventories among subsidiaries could be excessive. Under these conditions, each subsidiary may be unable to rely on others, and therefore may need to maintain a higher inventory level.

If an MNC has subsidiaries in foreign countries that are close together, the transferring of inventories among subsidiaries is worth considering. However, some countries require product specifications that differ from others. For example, each European country had historically established standards on some products that were different from those of other European countries. It can be costly to have inventories transformed in some way before being transferred among subsidiaries. In the late 1980s and early 1990s, European countries have attempted to develop more standardized specifications, which has resulted in the standardization of product specifications. Thus, inventories can be more easily transferred between these countries. If one European subsidiary experiences a shortage, it may be able to request inventories from another subsidiary in a nearby European country. Therefore, MNCs may be able to reduce the average amount of inventories held by their European subsidiaries.

Summary

Inventory policies are important because they can have a significant impact on costs and revenue of a firm. In general, firms attempt to minimize inventory while avoiding stockouts. To achieve this objective, firms must assess the future demand for their products. This task tends to be more difficult for MNCs because of global conditions that can affect demand, such as economic growth, exchange rate movements, their global production process, and trade barriers.

In addition to the decision of how much inventory to hold, firms must decide where to maintain the inventory. This decision is especially complex for MNCs with subsidiaries scattered around the world. Some MNCs make their subsidiaries responsible for maintaining their own inventories. Other MNCs have a centralized location which transfers inventories to subsidiaries upon demand. Some MNCs may allow subsidiaries to maintain a minimal amount of inventories, with either a centralized location or other subsidiaries serving as a reserve.

Discussion

The parent of Jordan Company produces medical supplies in the U.S. and exports them to firms in the United Kingdom. Its bulk shipments take about 12 days from the time that the order is received from the British firms. The British firms are charged a wholesale price in British pounds.

(a) Assume the other competitors are also located in the U.S. If there is a sudden expectation that the U.S. dollar will strengthen within the next three months, how will the demand for Jordan's supplies be affected?

Figure 19.1
Competition Between Jordan and Foreign Firms in British Market

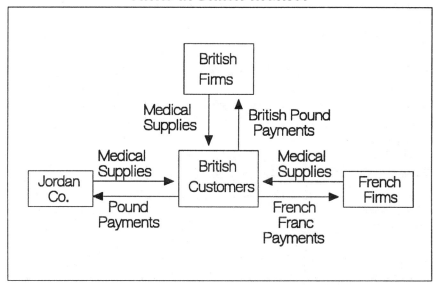

(b) Reconsider the previous example, but now assume that there are also firms in France that produce similar medical supplies as shown in Figure 19.1. What other information is needed to determine whether the British demand for Jordan's supplies will change?

(c) Would the cost to Jordan of carrying excess inventory be higher for its Canadian subsidiary or Japanese subsidiary? Why? (Assume the excess inventory can be maintained within the existing facilities at these subsidiaries.) What is the key factor that would cause the carrying costs to vary among countries?

20

Multinational Short-Term Financing

Firms that engage in international business commonly use foreign financial markets for short-term financing. Foreign subsidiaries of a multinational corporation (MNC) borrow from the local banks rather than from banks in their parent's country for the following reasons. First, their foreign subsidiaries may wish to establish a relationship with the local banks in case they need to request other services from the banks. Second, the foreign subsidiaries will typically need the local currency to support their operations, so that borrowing locally is more convenient. Third, they may be able to borrow at lower interest rates in the local country than if they borrowed from the parent's country, since interest rates can vary substantially across countries, as illustrated in Figure 20.1.

Using Foreign Financing to Hedge

In some cases, a subsidiary of an MNC will obtain financing from a different currency where interest rates are relatively low. If the subsidiary expects to receive some future cash inflows from its normal business

Figure 20.1
Short–Term Interest Rates Across Countries

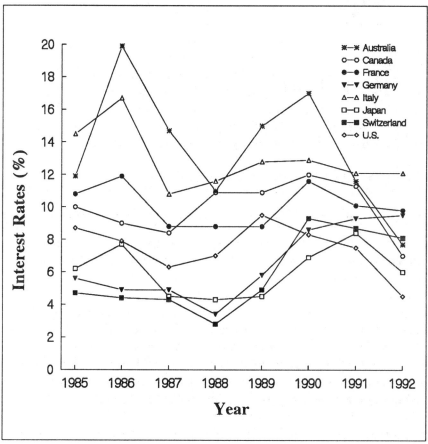

operations in this currency, it could use these proceeds to repay the loan. In this case, the subsidiary may be able to obtain funds at a low cost without being exposed to exchange rate risk. For example, if it exports products to that country, it could price the exports in that currency. The importers will normally be satisfied with this arrangement because they can use their home currency to make payment. If the subsidiary has borrowed funds denominated in this currency, it can use some of the cash inflows from the export sales to make interest payments on the loan.

Using Foreign Financing to Reduce Costs

A subsidiary may sometimes obtain short-term financing even if it does not expect to generate future cash inflows in that currency. Under these conditions, the subsidiary is exposed to exchange rate risk because it will need to convert its currency to the foreign currency it borrowed when it is ready to repay the loan. The expected financing rate to be incurred is:

$$r = (1 + i) \times (1 + e) - 1$$

where i represents the interest rate in the foreign currency borrowed and e represents the expected percentage change in the value of that currency relative to the subsidiary's local currency. For example, if a U.S. subsidiary planned to finance with Swiss francs at an interest rate of 5 percent annually and the Swiss franc was expected to appreciate by 3 percent against the dollar over the next year, the expected financing rate would be:

$$
\begin{aligned}
f &= (1 + i) \times (1 + e) - 1 \\
&= (1 + .05) \times (1 + .03) - 1 \\
&= .0815 \text{ or } 8.15\%
\end{aligned}
$$

If this financing rate is lower than the rate the subsidiary would have to pay in the U.S., the subsidiary may consider financing with Swiss francs.

Risk of Foreign Financing

The subsidiary must realize that the actual rate incurred from financing with Swiss francs could differ from what is expected. For example, if the franc appreciates by 9 percent against the dollar over the year, the financing rate for one year would be:

$$
\begin{aligned}
f &= (1 + i) \times (1 + e) - 1 \\
&= (1 + .05) \times (1 + .09) - 1 \\
&= .1445 \text{ or } 14.45\%
\end{aligned}
$$

If the franc depreciated against the dollar over the one year period, the financing rate would be even less than the interest rate charged on the loan. This can be confirmed by inserting any negative value for e (implying depreciation of the currency) in the equation to solve f. The logic behind this result is that the U.S. subsidiary borrowing francs would have converted the borrowed francs into dollars when the franc was worth more. If the franc weakens by the time of loan repayment, dollars can be converted to francs at a more favorable exchange rate. To illustrate, assume that the franc depreciates by 4 percent against the dollar over the one-year period. The financing rate over one year would be:

$$f = (1 + i) \times (1 + e) - 1$$
$$= (1 + .05) \times [1 + (-.04)] - 1$$
$$= .008 \text{ or } .8\%$$

In this example, the subsidiary's financing rate is very low because of depreciation in the currency that it borrowed against its home currency.

Since a currency's exchange rate can change substantially within a short time period, the actual financing rate from borrowing a foreign currency may be much different than the interest rate charged on that currency. During the Persian Gulf War in 1991, some European currencies such as the Dutch guilder, the French franc, the German mark, and the Swiss franc depreciated against the dollar by more than 10 percent in a single quarter. If a U.S. firm had borrowed foreign currency over this quarter, it would have experienced a negative financing rate. That is, it would have needed less dollars to repay the loan than the amount of dollars initially received when the foreign currency was borrowed and converted to dollars. Yet, there are also some periods in which these foreign currencies appreciated substantially against the dollar, which would have resulted in a very high financing rate.

Other Sources of Short-Term Financing

Many MNCs allow subsidiaries to borrow from each other. For example, if one German subsidiary is short of funds and another subsidiary has excess funds, a transfer of funds is appropriate. This method is more efficient than a bank loan because it eliminates the loan application process and transactions costs associated with bank loans.

If a German subsidiary needs funds and a French subsidiary has excess funds, the transfer of funds is complicated by different interest rates across countries. If the French interest rate exceeds the German interest rate, the German subsidiary may be better off borrowing from some source in its own country. The transfer of funds between subsidiaries of different countries is also complicated by exchange rate risk. That is, if the French franc appreciates against the mark over time, the number of marks needed to repay the loan would rise, increasing the German subsidiary's cost of financing. The German subsidiary would have to consider interest rate and exchange rate effects before borrowing from a subsidiary outside of Germany.

An alternative method of short-term financing for foreign subsidiaries is issuing commercial paper. For example, a German subsidiary that needs to borrow marks for 90 days could attempt to issue commercial paper in Germany. Common purchasers of commercial paper include individual investors, money market mutual funds, and other institutional investors.

Another possible method of short-term financing is by issuing Euronotes, which are short-term debt securities. Euronotes have a longer maturity than commercial paper, and have an active secondary market. They can sometimes be rolled over, and therefore may serve as a medium-term source of funds. When they are rolled over, the interest rate is adjusted.

Summary

Since MNCs frequently use short-term financing to support their ongoing operations, they can reduce their costs by making proper financing decisions. Some MNCs finance their operations by borrowing the foreign currencies that they will receive from future business, which acts as a hedge against exchange rate risk. Other MNCs borrow foreign currencies to capitalize on a low interest rate and or expected exchange rate movements. While this strategy can possibly reduce expenses, it may also result in higher risk.

Discussion

The parent of Jordan Co. needs to obtain funds for one year to support its U.S. operations, and is considering two alternatives as illustrated in Figure 20.2. It can obtain a loan in dollars at 10 percent, or a loan in Japanese yen at 8 percent. It expects that the yen will depreciate against the dollar by 2 percent over the year. If it borrows yen, it will convert the yen to dollars today, and convert dollars back to yen in one year to repay the loan.

(a) What is the expected financing rate from borrowing yen?

(b) Should Jordan finance with yen?

(c) How could Jordan involve its Japanese subsidiary in the payments arrangement to avoid the exchange rate risk from financing in yen?

Figure 20.2
Short–Term Financing Alternatives

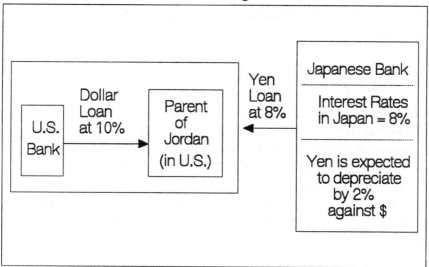

21

Estimating Cash Flows for Possible Foreign Projects

Developments in foreign countries have created numerous project proposals for U.S. firms. Some recent developments in Europe are summarized here to illustrate how they can lead to new foreign projects, but can also complicate cash flow projections.

Integration of EEC Countries

In the late 1980s and early 1990s, countries in the European Economic Community (EEC) removed numerous cross-country barriers. Regulations were standardized across countries and excise taxes on cross-border transactions were eliminated. These actions allowed for significantly lower costs of doing business across countries. Furthermore, firms with subsidiaries in several European countries became more efficient because their operations could be structured to satisfy one set of uniform regulations in Europe.

Impact of EEC Integration on Cash Flows

The cost savings could create positive cash flows for firms and encourage many firms to establish additional subsidiaries across European countries. These projects may have been unfeasible in previous years, but were being reassessed because of the cost savings involved. Some of the possible cost savings are:

(1) Reduction in marketing costs if marketing can be standardized across countries.

(2) Reduction in production costs if safety and environment specifications enforced by each country were similar.

(3) Consolidation of some tasks, since more standardized rules across countries eliminate the need for separate operations.

(4) Reduction or elimination of various taxes imposed on transactions across European borders.

The estimation of net cash flows resulting from any proposed project requires the measurement of expected inflows and outflows. The potential forms of cost savings described above reflect a reduction in expected cash outflows, which enhances expected net cash flows. Each possible form of cost savings must be assessed to derive a quantitative estimate of the reduction in cash outflows per year. The effects of EEC integration will vary substantially across proposed projects. Those projects that involve the transferring of products across borders of European countries will be valued higher as a result of the cost savings.

The integration of EEC countries can also affect expected cash inflows. On the favorable side, economic expansion caused by the EEC integration will overflow into many different industries. To the extent that the expansion enhances income levels and the increased income is spent by households, cash inflows of some firms will increase. In addition, the loosening of regulations allows some firms to provide financial services that were previously prohibited in some countries.

The integration of EEC countries could also have some adverse effects on expected net cash flows of possible projects. Firms must also recognize that their competitors are possibly considering European expansion as well. Thus, even though operations may be more efficient, competition could increase. This could reduce the forecasted sales generated by the project, and/or reduce the prices to be charged. Either effect results in lower cash inflows.

Possible Impact of a "Fortress Europe" on Cash Flows

The EEC integration was expected by some firms to cause a so-called "Fortress Europe," or a uniform set of trade barriers placed on products coming from outside of Europe. Therefore, multinational corporations (MNCs) may benefit from the increased efficiency of their European subsidiaries, but their European exporting business could be disrupted. Under these conditions, the net cash flows to businesses within Europe may be enhanced, but the net cash flows associated with the firm's prevailing export business may be adversely affected. If MNCs consider shifting more business to their subsidiaries to circumvent any possible "Fortress Europe" barriers, they must estimate the change in cash flows resulting from such a policy.

Impact of Free Enterprise in Eastern Europe

In 1989, the wall separating East and West Germany was torn down, allowing for eventual unification between the two sides. This led to a change in government philosophy throughout Eastern Europe toward free enterprise. Historically, numerous barriers prevented direct foreign investment in these countries and also prevented exporting to the countries.

As a result of the change in government philosophy, many firms began to consider expansion in these countries. With a more market oriented system, various projects could be considered that were previously not allowed by the host governments.

Free enterprise in Eastern Europe can affect the initial investment needed for a project there, the cash flows of the project, and the required rate of return on the project, as described below.

Impact on the Initial Investment

When the U.S. firms attempt to determine whether to invest in Eastern Europe, they will ultimately compare what they will have to invest to what they will get in return. If the initial investment requires the purchase of a subsidiary, the purchase price could be very uncertain because buildings and land were previously owned by the government, and have not been priced by market forces.

Impact on Cash Flows

For firms planning to expand their business in Eastern Europe, cash flow estimates for proposed projects are needed to determine whether the benefits from such projects exceed the costs. However, the estimation of a firm's net cash flows for projects in these countries is subject to much uncertainty for the following reasons. The estimated cash inflows are primarily derived from revenues, which are driven by demand. The demand for products in these countries is difficult to assess, as the products were not previously available. In addition, the income levels of people in the country are uncertain because of the movement away from complete government support. Therefore, even if the products were desired, there is some question as to whether the consumers could afford them.

The revenue would also be influenced by prices that could be charged for the products. Pricing policies are based on competition, which is difficult to assess for the future. They are also based on demand, which is very uncertain, as described above.

Cash outflows are primarily determined by expenses involved in the production, transportation, and marketing functions. Leasing costs are difficult to estimate because previous leasing and rent prices were set by the government, and were not market determined. Taxes are also uncertain because of the shift in government philosophy. Earnings to be remitted to the parent are subject to possible withholding taxes or currency restrictions.

The funds ultimately received by the U.S. firms as a result of doing business in Eastern Europe can be measured by first estimating the net cash flows to the subsidiary. As explained earlier, this task is very difficult. These estimates are then used to measure the amount of funds that will be remitted by the subsidiary in East Europe to the firm. The funds must be converted to U.S. dollars as they are remitted to the U.S. firms.

The future exchange rates between East European currencies and the dollar are difficult to forecast because these currencies have not been used frequently for international transactions. As the countries move toward free enterprise, the market value of their currencies may deviate substantially from their initially established values. Yet, even if the future market value of the currencies could be accurately forecasted, there is no guarantee that the currencies will be allowed to move according to market forces. The national governments could impose restrictions on the amount of currency that can be exchanged into other currencies. This would affect the equilibrium exchange rates, and therefore affect the cash flows to be received by U.S. firms doing business in Eastern Europe.

Impact on the Required Rate of Return

When comparing expected cash inflows and outflows of possible projects in Eastern Europe, firms need to establish a required rate of return for these projects. The required return would be based on the cost of financing the project. If some of the funds used to finance the project are to be borrowed locally, the firm must know the interest rate at which it can borrow before establishing a required rate of return. Yet, interest rates in East European countries were previously set by the respective national governments, and were not market determined. The actual equilibrium interest rate as determined by the market in any of these countries is difficult to estimate. If MNCs underestimate the cost of financing in these countries, they may mistakenly accept projects that will not recapture the financing costs.

Summary

In summary, numerous projects were considered for East European countries because of the potential opportunities to penetrate new markets.

While it is rational for firms to explore the possible opportunities, they must recognize that numerous other firms are considering similar opportunities. Therefore, any estimation of cash flows from potential projects must account for competition from other firms that also attempt to penetrate the European markets.

This example is not intended to discourage a firm from expanding into Eastern Europe or from estimating the cash flows resulting from a proposed project in a foreign country. It is simply intended to illustrate that cash flow estimation is subject to several sources of error. The complexities of international business tend to make international projects more susceptible to error. The chances of accepting a bad project or rejecting a good project are greater for international projects that exhibit these characteristics.

Discussion

The German subsidiary of Jordan Co. plans to promote its medical supply products in East European countries, in order to export the products (denominated in German marks) to firms in these countries. It will conduct a feasibility analysis to determine whether the exporting program would be worthwhile.

(a) Describe some of the key factors that will influence the cash flows to be received by the German subsidiary.

(b) Revenue from a particular type of medical equipment sold in East Europe could be forecasted by multiplying the forecasted price per unit times the forecasted number of units sold. Is there more uncertainty about the per unit price or the number of units sold? Explain.

22

Multinational Capital Budgeting

The general capital budgeting procedure for a foreign project is similar to a domestic project. Consider a U.S. firm planning to establish a store that will sell blue jeans in Mexico. The U.S. firm will compare the present value of expected dollar cash flows resulting from this store to the initial outlay (in dollars) to derive the net present value. If the expected net present value is positive, the firm may decide to implement this foreign project. While the general procedure is applicable to foreign projects, there are several international characteristics that need to be considered. These characteristics are discussed below, followed by a discussion of how capital budgeting techniques can be applied to account for the uncertainty of foreign projects.

International Characteristics Considered for Foreign Projects

The net cash flows estimated for this foreign project must account for the following characteristics that are not normally considered in domestic projects:

- foreign economic conditions,
- blocked funds and withholding taxes,
- exchange rate movements,
- effect on existing international business.

Foreign Economic Conditions

The sales level will be influenced by the economy in Mexico and potential competition there. These factors are not normally as critical to projects in the U.S. For projects in Mexico, a key economic variable to consider is inflation, since it has been over 100 percent in some years. To the extent that the store's costs and prices move with inflation, its earnings in pesos will be affected as well.

Blocked Funds and Withholding Taxes

Earnings generated by the store could be blocked by the host government for some period until they can be remitted to the U.S. parent. The timing of anticipated cash flows to the parent will be affected by such blocked funds restrictions. There may also be a withholding tax imposed by the host government on any earnings remitted to the parent.

Exchange Rate Movements

The peso earnings remitted to the U.S. will be converted at the prevailing exchange rate. Thus, forecasts of the exchange rate must be created along with forecasts of the peso cash flows in order to derive the dollar cash flows to be received by the parent. Exchange rate movements can have a major impact on cash flows. Consider that currencies of some industrialized countries have changed by more than 50 percent in some five-year periods. Thus, a given annual level of cash flows in some foreign currency could convert into a 50 percent change in dollar cash flows simply because of exchange rate movements. For less developed countries such as Mexico, currencies have sometimes declined in value by more than 70 percent in a single year.

It is sometimes suggested that any inflationary and exchange rate changes will have offsetting effects on a foreign project. Using our example, peso earnings could be boosted by high inflation in Mexico.

However, high inflation tends to place downward pressure on the local currency, so that the pesos would be converted into dollars at a somewhat unfavorable exchange rate, thereby offsetting the boost in peso earnings. While there is evidence of a relationship between the level of a country's inflation and the exchange rate, the relationship is not very precise, especially over the short run. Therefore, the exchange rate effects may be much larger or smaller than inflation effects, so that a perfect offset is unlikely. This means that firms considering foreign projects must explicitly consider potential inflation rates and exchange rates when assessing foreign projects.

Effect on Existing International Business

Another factor that should be considered is the effect of the foreign project on the U.S. firm's prevailing cash flows. For example, if the existence of the Mexican store reduces the firm's exports to Mexico (since customers can now buy the goods directly at the store in Mexico), the foregone cash inflows should be considered. It is possible for a project to be perceived as worthwhile when considered by itself, but be detrimental to the firm when considering the foregone cash flows at other existing businesses.

Summary of Factors Affecting Cash Flows of Foreign Projects

In summary, blocked funds and withholding taxes reduce the estimated cash flows and therefore reduce the foreign project's net present value. Depreciation of a foreign currency tends to reduce the net present value of a foreign project, since the initial outlay (in dollars) is converted when the foreign currency is relatively strong, while conversion of the foreign currency to dollars as earnings are remitted would be at a less favorable exchange rate. If the foreign currency of concern appreciated against the dollar, the conversion of foreign earnings to dollars over time would be at a more favorable rate, and therefore enhance the foreign project's net present value.

Accounting for Uncertainty in Foreign Projects

Given the various sources of uncertainty, it is obvious that the net present value resulting from a foreign project could be overestimated. Some international projects that are undertaken ultimately fail for this reason. Other proposed foreign projects may be rejected by mistake because their estimated cash flows were underestimated. Reconsider the previous example in which the sources of uncertainty are summarized below:

Type of Factor	How Factor Affects Value of Project	Factor is Influenced by
(1) Sales level	Affects peso cash inflows	Economic conditions in Mexico
(2) Prices	Affects peso cash inflows	Economic conditions in Mexico
(3) Costs	Affects peso cash outflows	Economic conditions in Mexico
(4) Blocked funds	Affects amount of funds remitted to parent	Rules imposed by Mexican government
(5) Withholding tax	Affects amount of funds remitted to parent	Rules imposed by Mexican government
(6) Exchange rate of peso	Affects amount of dollars received by parent	Economic conditions and possibly government intervention

Firms are well aware of the impact that the factors described above have on cash flows of foreign projects. However, it should be recognized that there is much uncertainty about these factors, especially those in less developed countries. Therefore, the estimated net present value of a foreign project is highly susceptible to error.

Since foreign projects are subject to some international circumstances (such as withholding taxes and exchange rate risk) not common to domestic projects, their cash flows are generally more difficult to estimate. With so many possible ways in which estimated cash flows of foreign projects are subject to error, it is necessary for firms to account for the uncertainty within the capital budgeting process. The capital budgeting techniques to account for uncertainty of domestic projects can be applied to foreign projects. However, the application is typically more complicated because of the characteristics peculiar to foreign projects. The more common capital budgeting techniques to account for uncertainty of foreign projects are:

(1) Use of a risk-adjusted discount rate.

(2) Use of certainty equivalents.

(3) Sensitivity analysis.

The application of these techniques to the Mexican project is explained below.

Risk–Adjusted Discount Rate

The risk-adjusted discount rate adjusts the rate used to discount cash flows for risk. The firm's required rate of return for most domestic projects could be adjusted to reflect a premium to compensate for extra risk on foreign projects. Since foreign projects may have different levels of risk, a different required rate of return may be applied to each proposed foreign project.

Even if the U.S. firm is considering the exact same type of business in various countries, there may be differences in risk across projects because of differences in country characteristics. For example, if the U.S. firm discussed earlier considered the project for Canada, the cash flows would vary from the project in Mexico because of differences in the: (1) demand by consumers, (2) prices, (3) costs (wages, machinery and leasing expenses, etc.), (4) taxes and other rules imposed by the host government, and (5) exchange rate movements relative to the dollar. The more uncertain these country characteristics are, the more uncertain would be the future cash flows resulting from the project in that country. Since the Mexican factors are typically more volatile than the Canadian factors, the cash flows of the Mexican project would be more uncertain. Therefore, the risk–adjusted discount rate applied to the project in Mexico would be higher.

There is no perfect formula for measuring the proper magnitude of discount rate adjustment to account for greater uncertainty on a foreign project. For example, even if it was known that the project's cash flows would be 20 percent more volatile than a similar project in the U.S., the discount rate adjustment is somewhat subjective. Once a risk–adjusted discount rate is determined, the decision of whether to accept or reject the project is simply based on whether its estimated net present value (NPV) is positive or negative. However, the magnitude of the NPV is based on the subjective risk adjustment to the discount rate. This implies that even if all managers agreed on the cash flow estimates for a given project and on the uncertainty of those cash flows, they may use a different risk-adjusted discount rate. Consequently, some managers may believe the project has a positive NPV and is therefore feasible, while others may believe the project has a negative NPV and is not feasible.

The firm's managers must be able to determine the additional risk premium that exists on risky foreign projects. In our example, the firm could attempt to measure the relative uncertainty of the Mexican project's cash flows to those of a similar project that has been implemented in the U.S. They could use the required return on the U.S. project as a base. That required return already includes a risk premium reflecting the characteristics of the project. An extra risk premium could be added to the foreign project to capture additional cash flow uncertainty caused by conditions in that country.

Certainty Equivalents

A second capital budgeting technique for capturing uncertainty is the use of certainty equivalents. Uncertain cash flows can be multiplied by a factor (called a certainty equivalent) that reduces cash flows to a level which a firm would be equally satisfied with if they were certain. For example, if one set of cash flows was almost certain, the certainty equivalent may be .9 or so, which implies that the managers would be equally satisfied with either the uncertain cash flows or 90 percent of those cash flows with certainty. A second project whose cash flows are very uncertain may have a certainty equivalent of .6 or so, implying that the managers would be just as satisfied with 60 percent of the estimated cash flows if they could receive them with certainty. Once the cash flows are adjusted to a risk-free perspective, they can be discounted at a risk-free rate to determine the present value.

In our case of the Mexican project, the certainty equivalents applied may vary over time. If Mexico's economic conditions or exchange rate movements are more uncertain in more distant years, the certainty equivalent applied to the project's cash flows in those years may be lower.

Like the risk-adjusted discount rate, the use of certainty equivalents will result in a single estimate of the project's NPV. Since there is no formula for applying certainty equivalents, there is some subjectivity involved, which will influence the estimated NPV of the project. Managers who are more risk-averse may use lower certainty equivalents than others, and therefore derive lower estimates of the proposed project's NPV.

Sensitivity Analysis

A third capital budgeting method to account for uncertainty is sensitivity analysis. This involves revising the estimated cash flows for possible scenarios that could occur. For the Mexican project, the cash flow is initially derived each year based on initial forecasts of cash flows according to particular economic conditions. Then, an alternative scenario is considered and cash flows are re-estimated. For each set of possible conditions considered, there is a unique set of cash flows, and therefore a unique estimate for NPV.

A simplified application of sensitivity analysis to the Mexican project is illustrated in Figure 22.1. First, different estimates could be developed for the sales level, prices, and costs, based on possible economic conditions that may occur. To simplify matters, assume that only two economic scenarios are possible. This results in two schedules of peso cash flows.

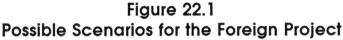

Figure 22.1
Possible Scenarios for the Foreign Project

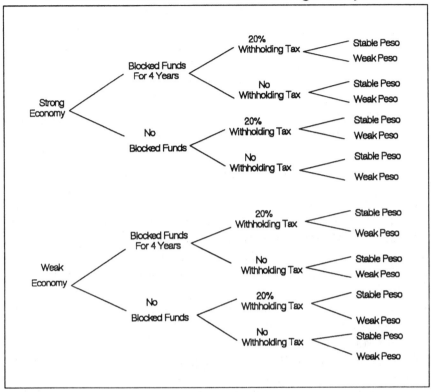

The next step is to determine the amount of pesos to be converted to dollars. There are some additional uncertain factors that must be accounted for. If blocked funds restrictions are uncertain, the peso cash flow schedules could first be assessed as if there were no blocked funds. Then the peso cash flow schedules could be assessed as if there were blocked funds for a specified number of years. The analysis could also account for uncertainty in withholding taxes by first assuming no taxes, and then redoing the analysis based on a specified withholding tax rate. These exercises will result in several possible schedules for the amount of pesos that will be converted to dollars.

The next step is to determine the dollar cash flows received from converting the pesos. This task is complicated because: (1) there are several possibilities for the amount of pesos to be converted to dollars, and (2) there are several possible future trends for the peso's value against the dollar. To simplify matters, assume that only two trends in the peso's value are considered. In this case, each possible schedule of peso cash flows would first be converted using the first exchange rate trend. Then, each possible schedule of peso cash flows would be converted using the second exchange rate trend.

In this example, there would be a total of 16 dollar cash flow schedules. If a probability can be assigned to each set of conditions, a probability distribution of NPVs can be developed. From this distribution, the firm's managers can decide whether to accept or reject the project. If the estimated NPVs for all scenarios were positive, the decision is simple. However, if NPVs for some scenarios were negative, the decision is more difficult. The managers may wish to determine the expected value of the NPVs (by summing the product of each possible NPV and its corresponding probability across all scenarios). They may also wish to assess the probability that the project will ultimately result in a negative NPV.

In some ways, applying sensitivity analysis may seem much more complicated than applying the other techniques to a proposed foreign project. Yet, the analysis can be expedited by using a computer spreadsheet. In addition, the analysis offers more insight than the other techniques about the probability that a proposed foreign project will be successful.

Summary

MNCs that assess the feasibility of foreign projects must consider international characteristics that affect the foreign project's cash flows, such as the foreign economy, government provisions on taxes and blocked funds, and exchange rates. MNCs must attempt to account for the uncertainty of foreign project cash flows. Capital budgeting techniques used to assess domestic projects can also be applied to assess foreign projects. These techniques attempt to capture the risk of a project by either adjusting the discount rate or periodic cash flows. The adjustment necessary for foreign projects may vary from the adjustment for domestic projects because they are exposed to international conditions.

Discussion

Last year, the U.S. parent of Jordan Co. had considered the development of a subsidiary in France, but decided that the project was not feasible. Since then, conditions in the U.S. and France have changed, so that the project may be reconsidered, even though the forecasts of French franc cash flows to be generated by the French firm have not changed.

(a) Last year the value of the French franc was forecasted to be somewhat stable. Now, the forecasts have been revised to suggest consistent appreciation of the French franc against the dollar over the next five years. Would this revision make the project more feasible or less feasible? Why?

(b) Over the last year, the long-term risk-free interest rate of the U.S. has risen. Would this revision make the project more feasible or less feasible? Why?

23

Global Cost of Capital

When firms use debt and equity (such as retained earnings) as their sources of capital, their cost of capital is based on the cost of debt and the cost of equity. The cost of capital of multinational corporations (MNCs) can differ substantially from the cost of capital of domestic firms because their capital is commonly obtained from numerous countries. A model for the cost of debt is developed below, and is then used to explain how the cost of debt can vary across countries. Then, a model for the cost of equity is developed, and is used to explain how the cost of equity can vary across countries. The discussion here carries relevant implications for MNCs that obtain capital from various countries.

Cost of Debt

The cost of debt can be measured as:

$$k_d = k_D(1 - T)$$

where:

k_d = after-tax cost of debt,
k_D = cost of debt before taxes,

T = corporate tax rate.

The before-tax cost of debt to the firm can be decomposed as:

$$k_D = k_{RF} + P_D$$

where:
k_{RF} = risk-free rate on long term debt,
P_D = risk premium required on debt by investors.

By substituting this equation into the previous one, the after-tax cost of debt can be written as:

$$k_d = (k_{RF} + P_D)(1 - T)$$

Thus, the firm's after-tax cost of debt is a function of the existing risk-free rate, the perceived risk of the firm, and the corporate income tax rate. Since these three characteristics can vary among an MNC's subsidiaries, the cost of debt varies among subsidiaries.

Differences in the Risk-Free Rate Across Countries

The supply and demand for loanable funds in any given country is partially segmented from other countries, because of several cross-border barriers such as exchange rate risk, and government restrictions on foreign investment. To avoid exchange rate risk, investors with available funds tend to invest them in the currency which they will need in the future. This segments each country's aggregate supply of loanable funds.

Similarly, borrowers prefer to borrow funds in the currency which their future cash inflows are denominated, so that they do not have to worry about exchange rate risk. Thus, the aggregate demand for loanable funds is somewhat segmented across markets.

Since supply and demand conditions are segmented, the equilibrium risk-free rates (which can be measured by monitoring rates paid by the national government in each country) are segmented by country as well. For example, the Japanese government can typically borrow funds in Japan at a lower interest rate than the British government can borrow in the United Kingdom, or the Canadian government can borrow in Canada. Japanese households tend to save more, which creates a relatively large supply of loanable funds in Japan, and is one reason for a relatively low Japanese interest rate. In addition, the expected inflation is generally lower in Japan, which can encourage households to save more funds there.

Since the corporate cost of debt is highly influenced by the risk-free interest rate, the cost of debt for subsidiaries in countries with a lower risk-free rate will likely be lower than the cost of debt for subsidiaries in countries with a higher risk-free interest rate. Risk-free interest rates for various countries are shown in Figure 23.1. Rates in some countries are substantially higher than others, suggesting that the corporate cost of debt may also vary across subsidiaries. Differences in the perceived risk premium and in the corporate income tax rate across countries can also cause costs of debt to vary across an MNC's subsidiaries, as explained below.

Differences in the Risk Premium Across Countries

If creditors across countries were asked to measure the proper risk premium that should be charged on loans to a particular firm, the answers may vary with the country of the investors. That is, creditors in some countries may require a higher risk premium on a corporate loan than creditors in other countries, perhaps because they are more risk averse. However, the differences in the risk premiums across countries is likely to be smaller than differences in risk-free rates across countries. Therefore, differences in risk premiums will not be as influential on differences in the cost of debt across countries, but should still be considered as a partial explanation.

Differences in the Corporate Income Tax Rate Across Countries

The third component of the cost of debt that can help explain why the cost of debt differs among countries is the corporate income tax rate. Since the corporate income tax rate varies among countries, the tax shield per dollar of pre-tax income will depend on where the subsidiary is located. For a given pre-tax cost of debt, a higher corporate tax rate

Figure 23.1
Risk-Free Interest Rates Across Countries

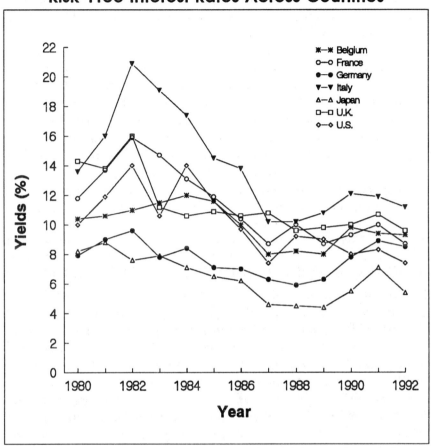

allows for a higher tax shield, and therefore a lower after-tax cost of debt. Thus, subsidiaries in countries with a higher corporate tax rate will incur a lower cost of debt, other things being equal.

Summary of Cost of Debt Components

Overall, the discussion above suggests that a subsidiary's cost of debt will be lowest if it is in a host country that: (1) has a low risk-free rate, (2) has a lower degree of risk aversion (which results in a small premium required on corporate debt), and (3) has a higher corporate tax rate. Since these three country characteristics can vary substantially across countries, the cost of debt can vary as well. This is relevant to the MNC, since it must recognize cost-of-debt differentials across countries (among other characteristics) when deciding how future corporate expenditures should be allocated across countries.

Cost of Equity

In addition to debt, subsidiaries also use equity (retained earnings) as a source of capital. The firm's cost of this equity (k_e) can be measured as:

$$k_e = k_{RF} + P_e$$

where k_{RF} represents the risk-free interest rate and P_e represents the risk premium on equity. Note that the risk premium on equity is not the same as the risk premium on debt (labeled P_D). Any equity funds of a firm ultimately belong to its shareholders. The shareholders should only be willing to let the firm make use of those funds if the firm's return from investing those funds is expected to equal the risk-free rate (which they could achieve with certainty by purchasing Treasury securities instead of investing in the firm), plus a premium that compensates them for the risk incurred.

Given that the risk-free rate varies among countries (as already explained), and a risk premium on equity could vary among countries (because of differences in risk aversion), the cost of a firm's equity will be influenced by the country where it is located. Therefore, an MNC's subsidiaries will incur different costs of equity, depending on where they are located.

Implications for an MNC's Cost of Capital

Since subsidiaries of an MNC incur different costs of debt and different costs of equity, they incur different costs of capital. Thus, an MNC is likely to have a different cost of capital than a purely domestic firm, even if other operating characteristics are similar for both firms. It is difficult to generalize about whether the MNC's overall cost of capital would be higher or lower than that of the purely domestic firm. Information about the countries of the subsidiaries would be needed to determine whether the MNC's cost of capital would be relatively high or low.

If an MNC issues stock only in its home country, its cost of the equity generated in this way is dependent on the risk-free rate and the risk premium at home. The earnings retained by the parent or any subsidiaries is another form of equity that has an opportunity cost. Since the retained earnings belong to the shareholders, it is expected that the parent or subsidiaries could reinvest the funds and earn a return that will satisfy the shareholders. The return should at least match what the shareholders could earn if they invested the funds themselves on a risk-adjusted basis. In other words, the retained earnings of the MNC's parent and subsidiaries have a cost equal to the risk-free rate plus a risk premium for the shareholders. If all the shareholders of a U.S.-based MNC are located in the U.S., the cost of the MNC's equity is somewhat insulated from conditions outside the U.S. This is quite different from the cost of debt, which is typically influenced by the countries where the subsidiaries are located. The difference occurs because the shareholders who supplied the equity are assumed to be in the U.S., while the MNC's creditors are located in numerous countries.

Consider a situation in which an MNC issued its stock in the U.S. and Canada. Even if the equity risk premium on the MNC required by U.S. investors and Canadian investors is the same, a portion of the MNC's cost of equity is still affected by the Canadian risk-free rate. In this case, the cost of equity is partially dependent on conditions outside the U.S. For MNCs that have issued stock across numerous countries, the cost of equity is partially dependent on conditions in all of these countries. As a general rule, U.S.-based MNCs tend to issue most of their stock in the U.S., but use significant debt financing from foreign countries. For these types of U.S.-based MNCs, their cost of capital is influenced by: (1) the MNC's cost of debt, which is affected by the risk-free rates, the risk premiums on debt, and the corporate tax rates in all countries where funds were borrowed, and (2) the MNC's cost of equity, which is affected by the U.S. risk-free rate and an equity risk premium.

Summary

Since MNCs commonly obtain funds from international markets, their cost of capital can vary distinctly from those of domestic firms. The cost of an MNC's debt obtained from a foreign country is dependent on the characteristics of the country. Thus, the cost of an MNC's capital will be influenced by the locations where the capital is obtained.

Discussion

(a) Assume that Jordan's foreign subsidiaries in Germany and Japan obtain most of their funds by borrowing from local banks. Assume that the risk premium on the debt is the same across countries, and the corporate tax rate is the same as well. Which foreign subsidiary would normally have the lowest cost of capital? Why?

(b) Jordan Co. is considering the creation of a new subsidiary which would either be based in Denver, Colorado or in Mexico City to produce and sell medical supplies in its local area. Either subsidiary would be financed with funds obtained from an issue of stock by the U.S. parent. If the Mexican subsidiary is established, the dollars would need to be converted to pesos. Peso earnings would be remitted to the U.S. parent. If the Denver subsidiary is established, the earnings would be periodically sent back to the parent. The expected annual dollar cash flows remitted to the parent would be about the same for the two projects. The investors will be informed at the time of the stock issuance whether the funds are to be used to finance a project in Colorado or in Mexico. Which project would likely have a higher cost of equity? Why?

24

Global Capital Structure Policy

It should be clear from any financial management text that the proper capital structure (mix of debt and equity) of a firm is dependent on the firm's financial characteristics. Domestic firms tend to use more debt when they generate somewhat stable or increasing cash flows over time. Thus, firms with stable or increasing sales are more able to handle a high level of debt. In addition, firms with assets that qualify as collateral have a greater borrowing capacity, and therefore may use more debt. There are several other factors that could also influence the choice of debt versus equity, which makes the capital structure decision difficult for domestic firms.

For multinational corporations (MNCs), capital structure decisions are even more complex. MNCs will normally borrow funds from the countries in which they conduct business. In this way, they can receive services from these institutions, such as cash management accounts, foreign exchange services, and economic advising services. Since the relative cost of debt varies across countries, an MNC's decision to use debt versus equity financing may depend on the countries where funds are accessible.

All subsidiaries of an MNC should not conform to the same target capital structure because they are subject to different conditions. Thus, each subsidiary may have a unique capital structure, since conditions in the host country of concern may favor proportionately more or less debt.

Factors Affecting the Capital Structure of Subsidiaries

Some of the more obvious factors that can cause an MNC's capital structure to vary across subsidiaries are:

- subsidiary earnings,
- exposure to country risk,
- cost of debt,
- exchange rate movements,
- agency problems of subsidiaries.

Each of these factors is described below.

Subsidiary Earnings

Foreign subsidiaries tend to obtain their equity funding from either retaining earnings or through an equity infusion from the parent. If the subsidiaries have recently experienced low earnings, and if the parent is unable to provide an equity infusion, the subsidiaries will be forced to rely on debt financing.

If a subsidiary's earnings are expected to be low or negative for several years, it may not be able to fully capitalize on the tax advantage of debt. Thus, it may consider using more equity, so that whatever debt is used can serve as a tax shield. Conversely, a subsidiary whose expected earnings are high would be more able to use debt as a tax shield, and may therefore prefer a more debt–intensive capital structure. While credits are commonly granted to MNCs whose subsidiaries paid foreign taxes, the tax rate may vary among countries, causing the tax shield of debt to be more effective in some countries.

Exposure to Country Risk

Subsidiaries are exposed to various forms of country risk, such as the possibility of expropriation. When subsidiaries borrow funds from local creditors, these creditors may pressure the host government to refrain from imposing any severe restrictions on the subsidiaries. It is in the interests of the local creditors to assure that the subsidiaries perform well enough to satisfy their debt obligations. Since country risk tends to be greater in less developed or developing countries, the subsidiaries based in these countries may be encouraged to use proportionately high levels of debt, so that they have the support of the local creditors.

A less severe form of country risk is a blocked funds restriction, in which earnings generated by the subsidiary are not allowed to be remitted to the parent until a specified future time. If a subsidiary anticipates that funds will be blocked, it may favor debt financing so that it can use more of its cash flows to cover debt obligations, and therefore will have a smaller amount of funds remaining that are affected by the restriction. The use of local debt precludes an equity infusion from the parent, and would favor a more debt-intensive capital structure.

Cost of Debt

Most subsidiaries that use some debt financing will borrow in the local currency where they are based. They can then use proceeds from their operations to cover debt payments without having to convert their cash to another currency before making payments. Given the existence of some cross-border barriers in financial markets, debt markets are segmented. Thus, the cost of debt tends to vary across countries. If the local cost of debt is relatively low, the subsidiaries may be encouraged to use a relatively large proportion of debt to finance their operations. Funding is not only low cost, but is unexposed to exchange rate risk, since future cash inflows can be used to repay the local debt. If many of an MNC's subsidiaries are in countries with low interest rates, the propensity for the subsidiaries to use debt could result in a debt-intensive capital structure for the MNC as a whole.

Exchange Rate Movements

Since subsidiaries will ultimately remit their earnings to the parent, they tend to monitor the exchange rate between their local currency and the parent's local currency. The MNC can benefit as a whole if the remittance of funds is timed to occur when the subsidiary's local currency is valued highly against the parent's currency. In this case, the remitted funds will convert to a larger amount of funds to the parent. While it is virtually impossible for the subsidiaries to know when its local currency has peaked, it may attempt to time its remittance when the local currency is relatively strong. In such periods, remitted earnings will be large, which means the subsidiary may have to rely less on equity (retained earnings) and more on debt to finance operations. Conversely, during periods when the local currency is weak, the subsidiary may retain all of its earnings rather than remit them, and therefore would need proportionately less debt.

Agency Problems of Subsidiaries

If subsidiaries can not be easily monitored by the parent, there may be an incentive for the subsidiary managers to act in their own best interests. To prevent such agency problems, the parent may request the subsidiaries to remit their earnings, which forces them to use a proportionately high level of debt to finance their operations. The subsidiaries would be monitored by the local creditors, and therefore are held accountable for their policies. In addition, the use of debt requires periodic debt payments, which reduces extra cash flow available to the subsidiary managers. Therefore, the agency problems can be reduced when subsidiaries use a high level of debt.

An alternative method for the parent to reduce the agency problems would be to have the subsidiaries sell some of the firm's stock to their corresponding managers, which may encourage managers to focus on maximizing the value of the firm rather than focus on their own self-interests. This method would result in proportionately more equity financing.

How Subsidiaries of MNCs Revise Their Capital Structure

As a country's conditions (such as country risk, exchange rates, etc.) change over time, the subsidiary's preferred capital structure may change as well. Subsidiaries can typically adjust their capital structure in the following ways. They can become more debt-intensive by borrowing from local banks or from their other subsidiaries, or issuing debt securities in financial markets. They can also become more debt-intensive by remitting their earnings to the parent, which causes their own debt-equity ratio to increase. They can become more equity-intensive retaining their earnings instead of remitting them to the parent, by receiving an equity infusion from the parent, or by reducing their outstanding debt.

In many cases, subsidiaries will gravitate toward their revised target capital structure by selecting the preferred type of capital when they need funds. For example, if they wish to become more debt-intensive because country risk has increased, they may remit more of their earnings to their parent, and borrow funds whenever they need them. A more abrupt method of achieving the target capital structure would be to borrow immediately, swap the proceeds for existing equity invested in operations, and transfer the equity to the parent. This abrupt method may only be considered if the subsidiary perceives an advantage to reaching the new target capital structure immediately.

Capital Structure Across Foreign Subsidiaries

Since conditions vary across host countries, it is possible that each foreign subsidiary may have a unique capital structure. For example, consider an MNC with two foreign subsidiaries. Assume subsidiary "A" has had low earnings recently and is in a country that has low interest rates and high political risk. Meanwhile, subsidiary "B" has had high earnings, but does not wish to remit any earnings to the parent at this time because the local currency is presently weak, and is expected to appreciate against the dollar in the future. These conditions may encourage subsidiary "A" to use debt financing, and encourage subsidiary "B" to use equity financing. The capital structure of the MNC overall would be somewhere in between the two extremes.

The disparity in capital structures across an MNC's foreign subsidiaries results from barriers that cause segmented markets. The existence of differential interest rates, tax rates, exchange rates, trade barriers, and capital flow barriers partially segments economic conditions between countries. Since a subsidiary's capital structure decision is influenced by economic and political conditions, and since these conditions vary across countries, each subsidiary's capital structure may be unique.

Why Capital Structures of U.S.–Based MNCs Differ From Foreign MNCs

While the capital structures of subsidiaries of U.S.-based MNCs are influenced by host country conditions, this does not imply that they are conforming to the capital structure of MNCs based in those countries. Firms whose headquarters are based in those countries may receive some forms of government assistance if they experience debt repayment problems. This could allow them to use a more debt-intensive capital structure. For example, some firms in Japan and West Germany can afford to use proportionately more debt because of more government support under adverse conditions. Furthermore, there may be financial support from other local firms that are suppliers or customers. This is somewhat common in Japan, where there are cross-holdings of shares between companies that serve each other. A financially troubled company may receive financial support from these other firms, because as large shareholders, it is in their best interests that the company survives.

While these country characteristics can allow firms based in specific countries to use proportionally more debt, these characteristics typically can not be applied to the subsidiaries of U.S.-based MNCs that are located in those countries. Financial support by the government or other firms is not likely for troubled subsidiaries of MNCs based elsewhere. Therefore, these subsidiaries may not be able to use as much debt as their competitors in the host country where they are based.

Summary

Since an MNC's subsidiaries are often located in various countries, the target capital structure will likely vary among subsidiaries. Debt financing may be favored by subsidiaries in countries where subsidiary earnings are high, country risk is high, the local cost of debt is low, and the local currency is strong (since they would remit more earnings). Equity financing is favored by subsidiaries in countries where subsidiary earnings are low, country risk is low, the cost of debt is high, and the local currency is weak. These factors specific to the host country of concern should be considered along with other characteristics about the firm to determine its proper capital structure.

Discussion

Jordan Co. attempted to use a capital structure for its foreign subsidiaries that capitalizes on the conditions in its host country. Consider the following information. Interest rates are high in Canada, moderate in Germany, and low in Japan. Country risk is not high for any of these countries. The exchange rate of the Japanese yen is expected to consistently depreciate against the dollar over time, while the Canadian dollar is expected to be stable, and the German mark is expected to consistently appreciate against the dollar. All subsidiaries need to raise capital at this time. The subsidiaries can either borrow long-term funds locally or receive an equity infusion from the U.S. parent, as shown in Figure 24.1.

(a) Based on the prevailing interest rates, offer recommendations for the capital structure of each foreign subsidiary.

(b) Based on the forecasted exchange rate movements, offer recommendations for the capital structure of each foreign subsidiary.

(c) Overall, what are your recommendations for each subsidiary's capital structure?

Figure 24.1
Alternative Financing Policies
for Jordan's Subsidiaries

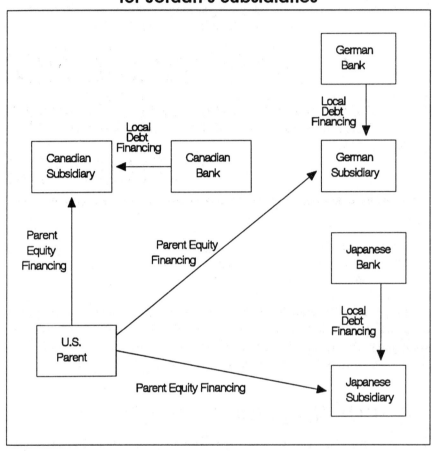

25

International Stock and Bond Offerings

As financial markets have become more integrated, multinational corporations (MNCs) have issued securities in foreign markets more frequently. First, the issuance of stock in international markets is discussed, followed by the issuance of bonds in these markets.

International Stock Offerings

In recent years, many U.S.-based MNCs have issued stock internationally rather than just in the U.S. The motivation for corporations to issue stocks in foreign markets is discussed, followed by an explanation of how MNCs promote the international stock offering. Then, the role of investment banks in international stock offerings is described.

Motivation for International Stock Offerings

There are several possible benefits from issuing stock overseas. First, an MNC may be able to create a global image by selling its stock in foreign countries. The MNC may be more able to sell its products in foreign countries if it has a global image. Second, it may increase the total demand for its stock by allowing foreign investors easy access. This could result in a higher stock price, which benefits the MNC's shareholders. Third, the MNC may improve its relationship with foreign governments, since it invites the local institutions to become shareholders. This may discourage the host government from imposing any types of restrictions or taxes that adversely affect the MNC's performance. If the host government imposed severe restrictions on the local subsidiaries of the MNC, the overall performance of the MNC would be reduced, and so would the stock price. Since institutional investors in that country that purchased the stock would be affected by these restrictions, they could pressure the host government to remove the restrictions. It is in the best interests of institutional investors based in foreign countries to assure that the MNC's subsidiaries in the host countries are treated fairly.

The MNCs that engage in international stock offerings already have some presence overseas, such as Delta Airlines and RJR Nabisco Holdings. Thus, the institutional investors in foreign countries may already be well aware of the MNCs, but previously refrained from purchasing shares sold in the U.S. because of the higher transactions costs. When the stock is sold in their countries, some institutional investors are more willing to purchase the stock. Thus, the MNCs can more easily create a foreign demand for their stock when they make it accessible in foreign markets.

How MNCs Promote International Stock Offerings

Representatives from MNCs planning international stock offerings travel to foreign cities such as London, Paris, and Frankfurt to make a presentation about their firm. The audience includes portfolio managers of insurance companies, mutual funds, pension funds, and other institutional investors based in these cities that may consider purchasing the stock. The representatives discuss various financial characteristics about the firm, such as reasons for recent performance of the local subsidiaries and the firm as a whole, plans for growth in various countries, plans for financing the growth, and expected future earnings. The presentation is intended to encourage institutional investors to invest in newly issued stock.

Role of Investment Banks in International Stock Offerings

The proportion of an international stock offering to be placed overseas is typically between 20 and 40 percent. An international syndicate of investment banks places the share with investors across various countries. In the past, there has been some concern about a so-called "flow-back" of shares to the U.S. as investors attempted to sell their shares. However, in recent years, flow-back has not been as prevalent, because other investors in these countries have been willing to purchase whatever shares are for sale in the secondary market.

The main underwriters for international equity issues include Goldman Sachs, Merrill Lynch, Morgan Stanley, and Salomon Brothers. Many of the larger commercial banks overseas such as Barclays are also actively involved, as they are allowed to engage in investment banking activities. Even some U.S. commercial banks such as Citicorp and J.P. Morgan are involved in such investment banking services outside the U.S.

The top ten underwriters of global debt and equity offerings are identified in Table 25.1. The top nine underwriters are based in the U.S. While there are numerous other underwriters, the top ten accounted for the underwriting of 71.6 percent of the value of all international offerings.

International Bond Offerings

International bond offerings by U.S. firms have increased substantially in recent years. The motivation for U.S. firms to issue bonds in foreign markets is described below. Then, the role of investment banks in international bond offerings is explained.

Motivation for International Bond Offerings

Like international stock offerings, international bond offerings can enhance the global image of firms. They also allow additional institutional investors to have a vested interest in the performance of the MNC. Since these investors expect to receive periodic interest on the bonds they purchase, they would be adversely affected by any host government restrictions that would severely hamper the MNC's performance.

Table 25.1
Largest Global Underwriters of Debt
and Equity in 1992*

Investment Bank	Value of Securities Underwritten Over First Six Months of 1992 (in millions)	Proportion of Total Global Underwriting
Merrill Lynch	$78,567	13.2%
Goldman Sachs	63,700	10.7
Lehman Brothers	57,428	9.7
First Boston	51,479	8.7
Kidder Peabody	43,613	7.3
Salomon Brothers	41,887	7.0
Morgan Stanley	34,303	5.8
Bear Stearns	25,519	4.3
J.P. Morgan	16,233	2.7
Deutsche Bank	13,251	2.2
Total for Top 10	$425,980	71.6%

*Source: Securities Data Co.

Therefore, they may help prevent the host government from imposing any unusual restrictions on the MNC.

MNCs that prefer to issue floating-rate debt may desire to issue international bonds in the Eurobond market, since these provisions are common in this market. In addition, they may prefer to denominate the bonds in a foreign currency, if the proceeds of the bond offering are to be used to establish or expand foreign operations. The periodic cash flows generated from these operations could be used to make interest payments on the bonds.

Not all firms would benefit from the international placement of stocks or bonds. To the extent that international offerings are used to create a global image or finance foreign operations, only those firms that conduct international business might benefit. Furthermore, firms typically need an established global reputation in order to attract sufficient international demand for their securities.

Role of Investment Banks in International Bond Offerings

An international syndicate of investment banks is formed to underwrite the bonds in the Eurobond market. There is no formal registration required. The issuance is initiated by the corporation, which contacts an investment bank to be lead manager of the syndicate. The lead manager helps create the international syndicate to place the bonds.

Security Offerings in the U.S. by Foreign Firms

Just as U.S. firms are issuing stocks and bonds in foreign countries, many foreign firms are issuing securities in the U.S. One reason for foreign firms to consider issuing securities in the U.S. is the large pool of U.S. institutional investors that may be willing to purchase the securities. Foreign firms that have some name recognition in the U.S. may be able to more easily place their securities in the U.S. than in their home market. In addition, they may believe that they can enhance name recognition in the U.S. by issuing securities there.

Foreign stock offerings in the U.S. have increased in response to the privatization of foreign firms that were previously state-owned. Some firms are unable to sell all the shares in their own country, and are therefore selling some shares in the U.S. To increase the liquidity of their shares sold in the U.S., some foreign firms have listed their stock on U.S. stock exchanges. This allows the stock to be traded in the secondary market on the U.S. stock exchanges

Foreign firms that issue stock in U.S. markets must meet Securities and Exchange Commission (SEC) requirements. Investment banks typically facilitate the stock offering process by developing a syndicate to place the shares in the U.S. Underwriting fees earned by the investment banks typically range from 3 to 6 percent of the offering.

Some of the stock offerings by foreign firms are privately placed with institutional investors in the U.S., such as insurance companies and pension funds. Based on Rule 144a, foreign firms that privately place their stock in the U.S. are exempt from some SEC requirements.

Some foreign firms have obtained funding from U.S. investors by issuing American depository receipts (ADRs), which are certificates representing ownership of the firm's stock. Firms that issue ADRs must meet specified SEC requirements. However, the requirements for issuing ADRs are less than those for issuing stock in the U.S. Thus, ADRs allow foreign firms to tap the U.S. market for funds without meeting all requirements associated with stock issuances in the U.S.

Summary

Given the motivation for some U.S. firms to place securities in foreign countries, and the motivation for some foreign firms to issue securities in the U.S., capital markets have become globally integrated. Barriers such as insufficient financial information can discourage some purchases of foreign securities. As this information becomes more accessible, global capital markets will be even more integrated.

Discussion

The German and Japanese subsidiaries of Jordan Co. need to raise long-term funds to support their plans to expand in their respective countries. They may issue bonds denominated in their respective currencies. Alternatively, Jordan's parent may issue stock denominated in dollars in the international stock markets, and distribute the proceeds to these two foreign subsidiaries. The two financing alternatives are displayed in Figure 25.1. The dollar is expected to strengthen against most currencies over the next several years. Any funds earned by each subsidiary after covering all expenses are remitted to the parent over time.

(a) Assuming that either alternative can enhance Jordan's global image, which alternative would be more appropriate?

Figure 25.1
International Stock versus Bond Offering

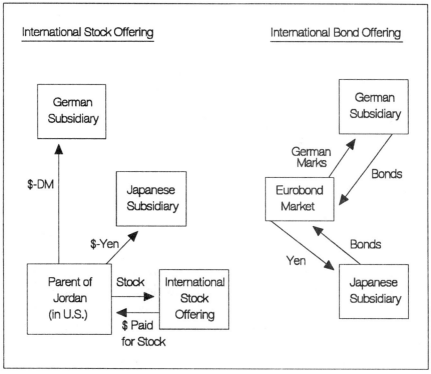

(b) Assume that the foreign subsidiaries will reinvest their earnings in their own country. Which of the two financing alternatives would result in higher cash flows after expenses for the foreign subsidiaries?

26

International Acquisitions

If firms and economic conditions were similar across countries, there would be no incentive for international acquisitions. The large volume of international acquisitions and mergers in recent years suggests that there must be some potential benefits to the combination of two entities from different countries. The value of foreign acquisitions of U.S. firms typically exceeds $4 trillion per year, while the value of U.S. acquisitions of foreign firms has been estimated at about $2 trillion per year. First, some of the more common motives for international acquisitions are discussed here. Second, the valuation of foreign targets is discussed, followed by a description of the impact of international acquisitions.

Motives for International Acquisitions

Some of the same motives for domestic acquisitions may also apply to international acquisitions, as described below.

Increased Efficiencies

One of the most commonly cited motives for domestic mergers is increased efficiencies, which may result from economies of scale or the elimination of redundant operations. Consider an international acquisition that allows for more complete use of the firm's existing production facilities. Firms with large fixed costs can sometimes increase efficiency (reduce the average cost per unit of output) if production is increased, because the fixed cost is spread over a large production volume. Some U.S. firms may be somewhat restricted from further domestic growth because they already have the maximum U.S. market share that the government will allow. Thus, they may use intentional acquisitions as a means of enhancing economies of scale. Even firms not restricted by the government may believe there is more potential for growth in foreign countries. To the extent that international acquisitions can allow for increased production at existing facilities, increased economies of scale are possible.

Some international acquisitions of firms in the same business may allow more efficiency, as only one accounting department, marketing department etc. may be needed for the combined firm. If redundant operations can be eliminated, costs are reduced, and the firm should benefit.

Some barriers may reduce potential gains in efficiency from international acquisitions. For example, differences in customs between countries may require different marketing plans in the two countries. In addition, differences in accounting regulations between countries may prevent consolidation of the two accounting departments. A customer service department may also be needed in each country so that customers in each country have easy access to service.

International Diversification

Another commonly cited motive for domestic acquisitions that may be applied internationally is diversification. To the extent that diversification can lower a firm's risk, the firm's cost of capital may be reduced. Some international acquisitions may cause the combined firm to exhibit less risk than the two individual entities because of diversifying a product line across regions. That is, the combined firm may be more capable of withstanding a recession. Consequently, an internationally diversified firm may be able to obtain funds at a lower cost.

There are some additional motives for international acquisitions that are not as common for domestic acquisitions, as described below.

Exchange Rate Expectations

A firm may attempt to benefit from a forecasted currency trend. For example, if a U.S. firm expected that the Canadian dollar would consistently strengthen against the U.S. dollar, it could purchase a Canadian firm today at a relatively favorable exchange rate. If the Canadian dollar strengthens over time, any remitted Canadian dollar cash flows would convert to increasingly larger U.S. dollar cash flows. In addition, if the Canadian firm is sold at some point in the future, the proceeds will convert to a larger amount of U.S. dollars, due to the strengthening of the Canadian dollar.

Differential Required Returns Across Countries

Another motive for foreign acquisitions is differential required rates of return. As an example, consider an Australian firm that is searching for an acquirer because it is experiencing financial problems. Given that the risk-free rate of interest in Australia is typically higher than in other industrialized countries, potential Australian acquirers would need a relatively high rate of return on the investment (acquisition) for it to be worthwhile. Therefore, they would only be willing to purchase the financially troubled firm at a low price. However, U.S. firms tend to have a lower required rate of return on acquisitions (which is primarily attributed to a lower risk-free rate in the U.S.). Thus, a U.S. firm may be able to outbid the potential acquirers, since it could possibly benefit more from the acquisition than the other firms. In essence, the Australian target would be financially supported by lower cost funds from the U.S., which increases the probability that the target could perform well enough to recover the financing costs.

This concept is often used to explain the numerous Japanese acquisitions of U.S. firms. During the 1980s and early 1990s, the cost of capital for Japanese firms was relatively low. Consequently, U.S. targets were more attractive to potential Japanese acquirers than to potential U.S.

acquirers. However, by 1992, U.S. interest rates had declined to their lowest level in over 20 years, thereby alleviating any cost of capital advantage for Japanese firms.

Positioning

Some international acquisitions may be intended to circumvent existing or potential barriers. For example, if any exporting firm expects trade barriers to restrict future exports, it may attempt to acquire a target in that country. In this way it can still serve the foreign market without being subject to trade barriers. As a related example, there was some concern that the integration among European countries would create a Fortress Europe, which would promote cross-country trade within Europe, but restrict exports from outside of Europe. Several companies from the U.S. and elsewhere acquired European targets to establish their position in Europe.

Valuation of Foreign Targets

Firms that consider purchasing foreign targets must assess the value of these targets. Since only a limited amount of financial data is publicly available, the firm may need to ask the potential targets for additional data. Some potential targets may resist, because they prefer not to be acquired.

The valuation procedure is complicated because of the different accounting guidelines across countries. Thus, the valuation procedure may need to be adjusted for targets in different countries.

Furthermore, consumer habits may differ across countries, which can influence the forecasts of future sales by a target that is acquired. For example, consumers in one country may view the target after the acquisition as they did before, while consumers in another country may switch away from the target after realizing that it is owned by a firm in another country. Such differences can affect the expected future cash flows and therefore the value of a target. Other country characteristics that can influence the valuation of a target include the financing rates in that country, government regulations on foreign acquisitions, and the expected future value of the local currency relative to the acquirer's currency.

Impact of International Acquisitions

As with domestic acquisitions, international acquisitions do not always fully achieve the benefits that were expected. In some cases, they may have an adverse impact on the value of the acquiring firm. For example, international acquisitions that were partially motivated by exchange rate expectations may fail if exchange rates move opposite to what was expected. Nevertheless, many international acquisitions have been successful and expedited the geographic expansion of multinational corporations. Thus, international acquisitions have facilitated the transfer of technology and innovation across countries.

Summary

International acquisitions can be motivated by increased efficiency, diversification, favorable exchange rates, or favorable required rates of return. The valuation of foreign targets must account for country characteristics such as financing rates, government regulations, and the expected local currency values. These characteristics influence the future cash flows of the foreign target, and therefore affect its perceived value.

Discussion

Jordan Company is considering the acquisition of a foreign firm in the United Kingdom whose stock is publicly traded and has a market value of 35 pounds per share. The U.S. parent of Jordan plans to pay for the British firm with its cash. The British firm will become a foreign subsidiary of Jordan, which would periodically remit earnings to the U.S. parent. Jordan expects that the British pound will consistently appreciate against the dollar.

    (a) How will Jordan's return on investment be affected by the exchange rate movements of the pound?

(b) Given the expected exchange rate movements of the pound, would Jordan benefit from purchasing the British target's stock now or deferring the purchase for a future point in time?

27

Global
Restructuring

Numerous multinational corporations (MNCs) have recently restructured their operations, including DuPont, Gulf & Western, IBM, Mobil, Rockwell, TRW, UAL Corp., and United Technologies. Senior financial managers may be assigned to assess various restructuring proposals and must therefore be able to measure the performance of individual divisions to assess each division's contribution to the corporation. The contribution of each division can be measured in terms of both return and risk. Some basic finance concepts about return and risk can be applied to evaluate restructuring proposals by MNCs, as discussed below.

Framework for Measuring Subsidiary Returns and Risk

The following framework can be used by senior financial managers to evaluate subsidiaries. The framework can be easily applied by any MNC, regardless of the number of geographic regions it serves or products it manufactures. When each subsidiary is assessed individually, a common proxy for return is the return on assets (ROA), although an alternative ratio may be more appropriate in some circumstances. The mean ROA over the periods being evaluated could be compared to assess historical profitability performance.

The standard deviation (σ) of each subsidiary's ROA would serve as a measure of each subsidiary's risk. To illustrate, consider the last 13 years of actual divisional ROAs compiled for a U.S.-based MNC. The return and risk statistics can be easily computed for each division with spreadsheet software, and are displayed in Table 27.1. Based on this table, the mean ROA is clearly highest in Europe, followed by Latin America. The standard deviation of ROAs is also highest in Europe.

Given that most MNC's headquarters incur some costs associated with foreign subsidiaries, the ROAs for foreign regions will typically exceed those of the home region. While this may distort the performance, each MNC can reallocate its costs to measure the financial condition of each region. This adjustment would normally boost the home region ROA at the expense of foreign regions.

The MNC can be viewed as a portfolio with each subsidiary representing a part of the portfolio, just as a stock portfolio is composed of individual stocks. Thus, the return and risk of an MNC is determined by its components. The MNC's return is simply a weighted average of all components. One measure of risk for the MNC is the variability in ROA, which is dependent on the: (1) proportional investment in each subsidiary, (2) variability in each subsidiary's ROA, and (3) comovements between subsidiary ROAs. Risk will be high for the MNC when the variability of

Table 27.1
Risk and Return Characteristics of Regions

Region	Mean ROA	Standard Deviation of ROA	Correlation Coefficients of ROAs			
			U.S.	Latin America	Europe	Canada
U.S.	8%	3%	1.00			
Latin America	14%	8%	.25	1.00		
Europe	16%	9%	.08	.60	1.00	
Canada	9%	5%	-.20	.28	.18	1.00

ROAs for each relatively large subsidiary is high, and when the movements in returns between these subsidiaries are highly correlated.

The contribution of each subsidiary to the risk of the overall corporation is especially relevant for restructuring decisions. As the composition of the portfolio of businesses run by the MNC changes, so does the potential ROA and risk. Consider how the variability of the MNC's ROA would change if the firm is planning to shift some of the corporate assets from Canada to the European subsidiary. The European subsidiary has had higher returns, but also has high variability of returns, and is more highly correlated with the returns of other subsidiaries. Thus, the risk to the MNC overall will be higher as a result of this type of restructuring. This restructuring proposition can easily be modeled on computer to measure the change in potential return and risk. As a second example, the divestiture of the Latin American divisions with the proceeds invested in the Canadian business would cause the variability of the MNC's ROA to decline, but may also cause the potential return to decline.

Restructuring to Optimize Asset Structure

To take this concept a step further, MNCs could attempt to determine their optimal asset structure, which reflects the proportional investment in each of their subsidiaries. Of course, each MNC has restrictions regarding labor costs, proximity to consumers, etc. and may desire that its investment in each subsidiary be no less (or no more) than a specified level. Thus, there may be constraints that reflect any minimum or maximum proportions invested in each subsidiary.

The optimal structure of an MNC is dependent on the risk preference of the firm's managers and shareholders. A firm that was not concerned about risk would consider 100 percent of foreign investment in the subsidiary with the highest expected return. However, when considering risk, other subsidiaries should be considered as well. In our example, the Canadian returns were lower than other foreign subsidiaries, but can effectively reduce the risk of the MNC. Its relatively low comovement in ROAs with the European division allow for substantial diversification benefits.

The optimal asset structure is not only dependent on the comovement of ROAs, but also how the ROA of one foreign subsidiary may be affected by the elimination of another subsidiary. Some subsidiaries offer services to each other, which may not be duplicated by external firms at the same cost. For example, one subsidiary may serve as the supplier for another subsidiary. Given their close relationship, the supplier may set a very reasonable price for supplies, and may assure immediate delivery. If the supplier subsidiary is eliminated, the costs of the other subsidiary may rise, and therefore the ROA may decline. Thus, the contribution of the supplier subsidiary to the MNC overall could be underestimated if its ROA was assessed without considering its relationships with other subsidiaries. The MNC should consider such relationships before making any restructuring decisions.

Restructuring for the Purpose of Positioning

Many forms of restructuring by MNCs are motivated by "positioning." The term "positioning" is used in various ways, but generally represents a strategy to revise the MNC's competitive position within the industry. For example, an MNC may restructure to eliminate subsidiaries that make up a very small part of the market share, and expand subsidiaries that already have a significant market share. This may allow the MNC to more fully benefit from its existing image. In this example, the restructuring allows the MNC to focus on its existing strengths.

In some cases, the MNC may believe that it has overinvested in a particular type of business, and may foresee a general decline in the demand for that type of business. Thus, it may restructure by shifting investment to a related business that can capitalize on its existing technology, and is more likely to grow over time. Restructuring by MNCs will continue to take place in response to changes in the popularity (demand) of certain businesses, the cost structure, regulations, and competition.

Accounting for Product Segments at Subsidiaries

Some firms may consider segmenting each subsidiary into product segments. If a firm manufactured two products at each of its five subsidiaries, it would have ten segments. The restructuring decisions would be based not only on the allocation of investments across countries, but also across products within each country. This approach is more appropriate than performing a geographical analysis separately from a product analysis. A firm may find that the foods segment of its Canadian division has negatively correlated ROAs with the foods segment of the U.S. division, even if the entire divisional ROAs of these two countries are highly correlated. This type of useful information could go unnoticed if product segments are ignored.

Summary

Financial managers of MNCs recognize that they must be able to oversee the inter-subsidiary relationships of the entire corporation. This requires a framework that measures the performance patterns of subsidiaries over time. An example was provided to illustrate how the framework can be used to assess restructuring policies. While the framework was applied here to assess a possible shift in investment from one subsidiary to another, it just as easily could have been used to assess the possible acquisition of a firm in another country, or possible expansion at multiple subsidiaries.

Discussion

Several years ago, Jordan Co. established the foreign subsidiaries because it desired to insulate its performance somewhat from the economic or industry conditions in the U.S. The U.S. parent of Jordan Co. recently assessed the return on assets (ROA) of each of its subsidiaries to measure their individual performance. It found that the ROAs of the Canadian and German subsidiaries were consistently high and somewhat similar to the performance of the U.S. parent itself. The annual ROAs of the Japanese subsidiary were not as high, and were independent of the ROAs of the other foreign subsidiaries. One executive of Jordan suggested that the Japanese subsidiary should be sold, and the proceeds could be invested in expanding the Canadian and German subsidiaries. The executive stated that this restructuring would retain the same degree of international diversification because the proceeds were reinvested in foreign subsidiaries.

(a) Why might the ROAs of one particular subsidiary be quite different from the ROAs of other foreign subsidiaries even when all subsidiaries produce and sell the same products?

(b) Do you agree with the executive's comments? Explain.

28

Currency Options

Just as options on particular stocks are available, so are options on currencies. A call option allows one the right to buy the underlying instrument while a put option allows one the right to sell the underlying instrument. A currency call option allows one the right to purchase a specified currency for a specified exchange rate (called the strike price or exercise price) up until a specified expiration date. The currency put option grants the right to sell the specified currency for a specified exchange rate up to a specified expiration date.

Currency options are available on widely used currencies such as the British pound, Canadian dollar, French franc, German mark, Japanese yen and Swiss franc. There are usually various contracts available, allowing some choice as to the exercise price and expiration date desired.

Speculating with Currency Options

Speculators purchase currency call options on currencies they expect will appreciate. For example, consider a British pound call option with a strike price of $1.60, and a premium (the price paid for the option) of $.03 per unit. Assume the spot (present) exchange rate is $1.59. If a speculator expects that the pound will appreciate to $1.67 over the next month, he could purchase a call option for $.03 per unit. If the spot exchange rate rises to $1.67, he could exercise the option, which allows him to purchase pounds for $1.60 each. Then he could sell the pounds in the spot market for $1.67 each, earning $.07 per unit more than he paid for them. After deducting the $.03 premium per unit, the net gain is $.04 per unit. Given that a standard British pound contract represents 31,250 British pounds, the transaction amount per contract would have been as follows:

Amount received by speculator when selling the pounds
= $1.67 x 31,250 = $52,187.50

Premium paid for the call option
= $.03 x 31,250 pounds = $937.50

Amount paid for pounds when exercising options
= $1.60 x 31,250 pounds = $50,000.00

Net gain
= $.04 x 31,250 pounds = $1,250.00

Speculators who expect that the pound will depreciate would consider purchasing put options. For example, assume that a put option on pounds with an exercise price of $1.60 has a premium of $.08. If the pound depreciates to $1.47, the speculators could purchase pounds in the spot market for $1.47 each, and exercise their put options, which allows them to sell the pound for $1.60 each. After deducting the $.08 premium, the net gain is $.05 per pound. The transaction amounts for a standard option contract on pounds would be as follows:

Amount received when selling the pounds at the exercise price
= $1.60 x 31,250 = $50,000.00

Amount paid for the pounds
= $1.47 x 31,250 = $45,937.50

Premium paid for the put option
= $.08 x 31,250 = $2,500.00

Net gain
= $.05 x 31,250 = $1,562.50

While these examples show gains from speculating in options, the obvious risk is that the currency's exchange rate moves in a direction opposite the speculator's expectations. In this case, the speculator may have to let the option expire without exercising it, which results in a loss of the premium paid for the option.

For every buyer of an option, there has to be a seller. Speculators who sell call options take the position opposite to the buyers of call options. Thus, they expect that the currency will either depreciate (or at least not appreciate substantially). They receive the premium paid for the call option. If the call option is not exercised, they earn the premium. If the currency call option is exercised, they are obligated to sell to the owner the currency specified in the options contract at the specified exercise price.

Using the currency call option example discussed earlier, assume that the seller of the call option planned to obtain the currency only at the time the call option was exercised. In this case, the seller of the call option would have paid $1.67 for pounds in the spot market, and then sold those pounds to the owner of the call option for $1.60 per pound. After accounting for the $.03 initially received by the seller of the call option, the net gain is -$.04 per unit, which reflects a loss of $1,250 for one standard contract. In the absence of transactions costs, the loss (gain) to the seller would equal the gain (loss) to the buyer of the currency call option.

Sellers of currency put options receive a premium in exchange for their obligation to buy the currency specified in the contract at the specified exercise price at the time the owner of the put option exercises the option. Sellers of currency put options typically expect that the currency of concern will not depreciate by much, if at all. In the earlier example on the put options, the sellers of the pound put option would have received a $.08 premium per unit. However, they would have paid $1.60 for the pound at the time the option was exercised. If they sold the pounds in the spot market at that time, they would have received $1.47 (which was the spot rate) which is $.13 lower than the price they paid for pounds. After accounting for the $.08 premium received, their loss would be $.05 per unit. Assuming that they immediately sell the currency received at the time the option was exercised, their loss (gain) should equal the put option owner's gain (loss).

Factors Affecting Currency Option Premiums

The premium paid for currency call options is mainly determined by three factors. First, the higher the spot rate relative to the exercise price, the higher is the premium. Second, the longer the time to the expiration date, the higher is the premium. Third, the greater the currency's volatility, the higher the premium. Each of these factors can influence the probability of the option being exercised and the magnitude of the gain from exercising the option. While these factors are beneficial to the buyer, sellers of call options will require a higher premium to compensate.

The premium paid for currency put options is mainly determined by the same three factors. This first factor, spot exchange rate relative to exercise price, affects a put option in the opposite manner. The higher the spot rate relative to the exercise price, the lower is the premium (since such conditions are unfavorable to the owner of a put option). The other two factors have a similar relationship with put option premiums as was mentioned for call option premiums.

Hedging with Currency Options

Since currency options can lock in the future exchange rate of a specified currency, they are commonly used by MNCs to hedge international transactions. Currency options can be used to hedge the following types of international transactions:

- importing,
- exporting,
- foreign acquisitions,
- remitted earnings.

The use of currency options to hedge each type of transaction is explained below.

Importing

Currency options are sometimes used by corporations to hedge future cash outflows denominated in foreign currencies. For example, if a U.S. importing firm ordered supplies from France that were to be paid for in francs three months from now, it could buy call options on francs. This would lock in the maximum amount the firm would have to pay for francs. If the spot rate of the franc in three months was less than the exercise price, the firm would let the options expire and purchase the francs in the spot market.

Exporting

Firms that receive payments in foreign currencies can purchase currency put options to hedge future cash inflows denominated in foreign currencies. For example, if a U.S. exporting firm expected to receive a payment denominated in German marks, it could hedge that position by purchasing put options on marks. This would allow the firm to sell the marks received at a specified exchange rate, which effectively locks in a minimum amount of dollars to be received when converting the marks. If the spot rate of the mark was higher than the exercise price at the time the marks were received, the firm would let the options expire and sell the marks in the spot market.

Foreign Acquisitions

Consider a U.S.-based MNC which plans to acquire a British firm. The MNC's parent has bid for the British firm and plans to use cash to purchase the shares. However, since there are other bidders for this firm, the MNC will not know if it is the winning bidder until one month from now. Assume the MNC expects the British pound to appreciate against the dollar. If it knew that it would be the winning bidder, it would prefer to lock in the exchange rate of the pound now. However, it does not want to take a position in pounds unless it is sure it will need them to make the acquisition. Under these conditions, the MNC could hedge its position by purchasing call options on pounds. If it turns out to be the winning bidder, the call options lock in the maximum price paid for pounds. Should the spot rate of the pound be less than the exercise price from the option, the MNC would simply purchase pounds at the spot rate and would not exercise the option.

If the MNC was not the winning bidder, it may still exercise the call option if the pound's spot rate exceeds the exercise price at some point before the option expires. Even though the MNC would not need the pounds, it could reconvert them back to dollars at the prevailing spot rate.

An alternative hedge in this example is the forward purchase, which locks in the exchange rate for a specified currency at a specified date. However, since the forward purchase is an obligation, the MNC would be forced to exchange dollars for pounds at the specified future date, even if it was not the winning bidder. The call option provides more flexibility because the MNC is not obligated to exercise the option. Of course, the MNC should also consider that a premium must be paid for the currency call option. If the MNC did not expect the pound to appreciate over the next month, it would probably not hedge at all. The call option essentially serves as protection in the event that the pound does appreciate. The MNC must decide whether the insurance provided by the options is worth the cost.

Remitted Earnings

When foreign subsidiaries of U.S.-based MNCs remit their funds to the parent, the amount of dollars received by the parent is dependent on the exchange rate at that time. If a parent is concerned that the foreign currency will depreciate against the dollar, it could purchase put options on the foreign currency that will be converted to dollars in the future. For example, if the parent anticipated that it would receive 1 million Swiss francs nine months from now, it could purchase put options on Swiss francs with an expiration date of nine months from now.

An alternative approach would be to sell Swiss francs forward with a forward contract. However, it must recognize the tradeoff involved. The forward contract is a cheaper way to hedge, but does not allow as much flexibility. If the Swiss franc appreciated by the time the earnings were remitted, the MNC would have been better off without a hedge. If it used a put option to hedge, it could let the contract expire, whereas if it used the forward contract, it would have to fulfill its obligation.

Inter-Subsidiary Transactions

As subsidiaries of an MNC that are based in different countries sell supplies or materials to each other, payments are made by one subsidiary to the other. When there are frequent shipments between a U.S. subsidiary and a foreign subsidiary, payments may be "netted" out to determine the net amount one subsidiary owes the other at the end of each month. If the U.S. subsidiary is making the end-of-month payment, and anticipates that the dollar will depreciate against the foreign subsidiary's currency, it may decide to hedge its future payment by purchasing call options on the currency it will need. As with all other situations, it could hedge at a lower cost by using a forward contract (purchasing the foreign currency forward in this case), but there is less flexibility with the forward contract.

Summary

Currency options are used by MNCs to hedge future cash flows in foreign currencies. They allow more flexibility than forward contracts, and therefore can be beneficial when the firm is uncertain about future exchange rates. While currency options can be expensive, their flexibility can be worth the cost.

Discussion

The Japanese subsidiary of Jordan Co. periodically remits some earnings to the U.S. parent. Executives of Jordan are concerned about earnings to be remitted in six months, because they anticipate that the yen will depreciate substantially against the dollar by then.

   (a) Explain how Jordan could hedge this transaction with currency options.

(b) What is a possible advantage of this hedge versus a forward sale of yen?

(c) What is a possible disadvantage of this hedge versus a forward sale of yen?

29

Integrated Multinational Financial Management

This case study on Spark Company reflects the dilemmas commonly faced by U.S. firms that conduct international business. The case requires an understanding of many of the concepts that were discussed throughout this text.

Spark Co. is a U.S.-based multinational corporation that produces sport shirts. The shirts are produced in a plant in Florida, and sent to distribution subsidiaries in five cities in the U.S., and in London, England. These subsidiaries are responsible for marketing the shirts in their respective cities and selling them to local retail stores. The plant charges the subsidiaries a price that is based on costs of producing the shirts and transporting them to the subsidiaries, plus a small markup. The subsidiaries price the shirts based on the price they pay plus their costs of marketing the shirts, plus a small markup.

The distribution subsidiary based in Detroit exports shirts in bulk to some Canadian stores. The exports are denominated in U.S. dollars, and priced to account for the transportation costs. The plant in Florida charges all of its subsidiaries the same price for its shirts, except that transportation costs incurred by subsidiaries vary. The shirts transported from the plant to the British subsidiary are denominated in U.S. dollars.

Spark Co. has been successful over the years by specializing only on the production of high-quality shirts, undercutting the prices of other substitute high-quality shirts that are produced locally in the three countries, and relying on large sales volume. Their relatively low price has been the key to their success. While the shirts are high-quality, they are not perceived as different from many other high-quality brands that are produced locally in each of the three countries. Spark Co. has maintained a high level of efficiency through specialization, and therefore has little room for improvement in that respect. The plant is not fully utilized, but would be if production was increased by about 20 percent.

The profile of typical customers is men between 25 and 35 years old with above-average income levels. The demand for the shirts appears to be insensitive to changes in national income, but very sensitive to changes in the price charged to customers.

Spark's forecast for the remainder of the 1990s is that the economies of the three countries would improve, as the gross national product should increase by 4 percent per year in each country. The inflation rates of the U.S., Canada, and England will be about 2 percent a year.

Interest rates are higher in England than in Canada or the U.S. The U.S. interest rate is forecasted to be relatively low throughout the remainder of the 1990s. Conversely, interest rates in England are expected to rise substantially throughout the 1990s. While exchange rate forecasts are subject to error, the managers of Spark Co. are quite confident that the Canadian dollar and British pound will depreciate at least 3 percent per year against the dollar.

Discussion

Answer each of the following questions independently (without considering any possible policies stated in the other questions).

(a) Assuming that Spark Co. does not change its marketing strategy, will the Canadian demand for Spark shirts increase or decrease? What about the British demand for Spark shirts? Explain.

(b) Would Spark benefit from lowering the prices of its shirts to increase the demand?

(c) Assume that the profit margin at Spark's production plant has been insensitive to exchange rate movements. Does this imply that Spark's stock price has been insensitive to exchange rate movements? Explain.

(d) Assuming that Spark intends to continue specializing only in the production of high-quality shirts, should it adjust its efforts in marketing the shirts in the three different countries, given the forecasts for the remainder of the 1990s?

(e) Spark was concerned that the profitability of its British subsidiary was somewhat volatile over time, and considered diversifying its exports to several regions in England, rather than focusing on London. Would this diversification strategy reduce the firm's risk?

(f) Explain why Spark Co. might consider hedging its exchange rate risk resulting from its British business. If it decides to hedge one year ahead, it has a choice of selling a one year forward contract at $1.70, or buying a one year put option with an exercise price of $1.70 with a premium of $.03. The spot exchange rate is $1.70. Which type of hedge is more appropriate for Spark?

(g) Assume Spark has been considering whether to invest its excess cash in British Treasury bills at 9 percent, or in U.S. Treasury bills at 8 percent. Assume a one-year investment period, and no default risk for either investment. Which investment is more feasible?

(h) Assume that Spark needs short-term funds to support its U.S. operations. It can either: (1) borrow $1.7 million for one year at 9 percent, or (2) borrow 1 million pounds at 10 percent, and convert them to the $1.7 million that is needed to support its U.S. operations, but the loan repayment in one year must be in pounds. Which alternative appears to be less costly? Which alternative is more feasible when accounting for the expected cost and the uncertainty?

(i) Several managers of Spark Co. were requested by the chief financial officer (CFO) to consider the possibility of establishing a small plant in England that would produce the shirts there. Spark Co. presently has $8 million in excess cash that could be used to establish the plant. The shirts would then be distributed directly from the plant to retail stores. The CFO felt that this strategy could reduce the exposure to exchange rate risk since the costs of production would be in the same currency as the revenues generated from selling shirts in England. Any revenues beyond costs would be remitted to the U.S. Would the overall performance of Spark Co. be less exposed to exchange rate risk as a result of this strategy? Offer some general insight as to whether a capital budgeting analysis would support the establishment of a subsidiary in England.

(j) If Spark Co. established a British plant, how would the British translated earnings be affected by the expected change in the value of the British pound?

(k) If Spark Co. established a British plant, how could it attempt to hedge the translation effects? Should it hedge the translation effects?

(l) Assume that Spark Co. establishes a British plant to produce shirts, and that the operations are financed with local loans from British banks. Assume the inventory maintained at the British plant was the same as the inventory maintained at the U.S. plant. Explain why the costs of carrying these inventory are not the same for both plants.

Answers to End-of-Chapter Discussion Questions

Chapter 1

(a) Some of Jordan's more obvious financial decisions related to international business include:
   (1) whether to expand its foreign subsidiaries,
   (2) how much of the earnings of foreign subsidiaries should be remitted to the parent,
   (3) whether to establish subsidiaries in other countries,
   (4) how should the foreign subsidiaries finance any expansion,
   (5) how should the foreign subsidiaries invest their excess cash.
   Many other financial decisions could also be considered here.

(b) Jordan Co. may attempt to establish a subsidiary in Mexico or Eastern Europe to produce the supplies (to capitalize on lower wage rates). Alternatively, it may consider selling medical supplies in those countries.

Chapter 2

(a) The agency costs are higher for the Japanese subsidiary because the parent would have more difficulty monitoring the Japanese subsidiary. This is because: (1) the subsidiary's distance from the U.S. discourages frequent visits by the parent's executives, (2) the customs of Japan are substantially different for the Japanese managers that may manage the Japanese subsidiary, (3) the language differences may hamper any monitoring by the parent.

(b) The Canadian subsidiary's earnings would be enhanced by appreciation of the Canadian dollar when translated to U.S. dollars, while the Japanese subsidiary's earnings would be reduced by the yen's depreciation when translated to U.S. dollars. Thus, the Canadian subsidiary's performance would be higher. If the translation effect was not considered, the managers of the Canadian subsidiary may be able to make decisions that serve their own interests, since the reported profitability in U.S. dollars would be enhanced by the translation effect, and therefore could hide any financial problems.

(c) Even if the Japanese subsidiary may generate high earnings in yen, the U.S.-based MNC's shareholders may not benefit because: (1) the conversion of yen to U.S. dollars as earnings remitted to the parent may result in a low level of U.S. earnings received if the yen depreciates against the dollar, and (2) extra taxes may need to be paid on any earnings remitted.

Chapter 3

(a) Jordan's subsidiary earnings may be taxed by each host government. Then the cash flows to be remitted by the subsidiary may be subject to a withholding tax. There may even be a tax imposed by the U.S. government. The cash flows to the parent are influenced by all of the effects described above.

(b) If Germany's tax laws result in higher taxes, Jordan's after-tax cash flows will be reduced. Jordan may shift some if its German operations to other countries to avoid the high taxes.

Chapter 4

(a) The high budget deficit will place upward pressure on German interest rates. The high inflationary expectations will place upward pressure on Canadian interest rates. The shift in Japanese savings should place downward pressure on Japanese interest rates and upward pressure on U.S. interest rates.

(b) Jordan's sales will likely increase in Japan, but decrease in Canada, Germany, and the U.S. Thus, its aggregate level of sales will likely be reduced by the events.

Chapter 5

(a) Jordan's subsidiaries will periodically convert Canadian dollars, German marks, and Japanese yen to U.S. dollars as earnings are remitted to the U.S. parent. The U.S. parent will periodically convert pounds to dollars as it receives payments for British exports. The U.S. parent will periodically convert dollars to pesos to pay for Mexican imports.

(b) Jordan's subsidiaries will periodically deposit funds at Eurobanks in the Eurocurrency market. They will also periodically borrow short-term funds from these banks in the Eurocurrency market, or borrow intermediate-term funds in the Eurocredit market.

Chapter 6

(a) The probability distribution of the dollars to be received is:
   $1,700,000; 30% probability
   $1,750,000; 50% probability
   $1,800,000; 20% probability

(b) The expected value of the dollars to be received is:
   $1,700,000 (30 percent) + $1,750,000 (50 percent)
       + $1,800,000 (20 percent)
   = $510,000 + $875,000 + $360,000
   = $1,745,000

(c) The probability that Jordan will benefit from hedging is 30 percent (which occurs under the scenario in which the pound's exchange rate in one year is $1.70).

(d) This answer involves a risk–return tradeoff. Most firms would likely prefer to remain unhedged, since there is a good chance of receiving a higher dollar amount by not hedging. Firms with a very high degree of risk aversion may prefer to hedge.

Chapter 7

(a) The standard deviation of the ROA for Jordan's consolidated operations should be lower than that of each foreign subsidiary's ROA, as long as the ROA cycles across subsidiaries are not highly correlated.

(b) The ROA of the consolidated operations would be affected under these conditions, because the weights (proportion of total investment) allocated to the foreign subsidiaries have changed. The covariances of ROAs between foreign subsidiaries are likely different. So when the new weights are applied, the portfolios's (total MNC's) standard deviation of ROAs would be affected.

Chapter 8

(a) Economic conditions in Canada tend to be somewhat similar to those in the U.S. Thus, the Canadian subsidiary is indirectly affected by the U.S. economic conditions. The economic conditions of Germany and Japan may also be related to economic conditions of the U.S. but the relationship is typically not as strong.

(b) The production costs of Jordan's British business is based on economic conditions (wage rates, leasing expenses, etc.) in the U.S. However, the British demand for the products is somewhat dependent on economic conditions in the United Kingdom (such as national income and the strength of the British pound).

Chapter 9

(a) If the businesses have similar performance, it would appear that market conditions are not segmented.

(b) If the facility is established in the U.S., the sensitivity of the MNC to U.S. economic conditions should increase. Therefore, the domestic beta should increase.

If the facility is established in Canada, the domestic beta may decrease slightly. However, if the Canadian and U.S. economies are very integrated, the new Canadian business is not really insulated from the U.S. market.

If the facility is established in New Zealand, the domestic beta should decline because the business would likely be somewhat insulated from U.S. market conditions (as long as there is some segmentation between the U.S. and New Zealand markets).

Chapter 10

(a) Disagree. If the pound appreciates against the franc, British customers will be able to obtain supplies from France for less pounds than what was required before. Thus, they may shift away from U.S. firms in favor of French firms, causing a decline in Jordan's export business.

(b) Assuming that British customers view the supplies produced by the firms as adequate substitutes for each other, they may switch away from French and U.S. firms in favor of British firms, because the pounds needed to purchase supplies from the French and U.S. firms would have increased due to the exchange rate movements. Thus, Jordan's cash flows from exports may decline, and its value will decline as well.

Chapter 11

(a) The perceived value would be reduced, because any dividend payments will convert to smaller dollar amounts.

(b) Jordan should consider deferring the purchase until after the franc depreciates so that it could purchase francs at a more favorable rate before purchasing shares of the French firm.

Chapter 12

(a) The German mark-denominated bond's value moves inversely with German interest rates. Thus, the bond value should rise in response to a decrease in German interest rates.

(b) The mark-denominated coupon payments would convert to higher dollar amounts over time, due to the mark's appreciation against the dollar.

Chapter 13

(a) The historical sales figures are based on the amount of each product sold, and the prices of each product. As economic conditions (such as economic growth and inflation) change, so will the amount sold and the prices charged. Second, the prices of products were typically set by the government and therefore were not market determined. The shift toward a market oriented system will cause an adjustment in the prices to be charged. Third, competition will result from a movement toward free enterprise, which will affect future sales.

(b) The historical expenses will change because wages and costs of equipment will be determined by market forces rather than by the government. Also, the costs of leasing the facility must be estimated if the government retains ownership.

(c) Investors may be discouraged from purchasing the company because of the uncertainty about Hungary's price levels, wage levels, competition, etc. Thus, if Jordan did a more thorough analysis, it may believe that other investors are overreacting to the uncertainty. It may be able to purchase the company at a very low price because other potential bidders are unwilling to take the risk.

Chapter 14

(a) The translation of long-term debt of foreign subsidiaries will result in an abnormally low consolidated level of long-term debt when foreign currencies are weak (when the U.S. dollar is strong). Thus, if the firm's debt-equity ratio is relatively high compared to domestic firms, it must have an unusually high level of debt. Once the foreign currencies regain some strength, this will become more obvious.

(b) The debt-equity level may be lower than in previous years because of the translation effect. The consolidated debt level is lower when foreign currencies are weaker.

Chapter 15

(a) Jordan's overall performance would be affected by international conditions such as the economic conditions, industry conditions, exchange rates, taxes, and competition in the countries where it conducts international business.

(b) The British demand for Jordan's exports could be influenced by economic conditions in the United Kingdom, such as the growth in national income.

   If foreign firms were competing in the medical supplies market in the U.S., the U.S. parent would have to monitor international conditions such as foreign wage rates (which affect production costs) and exchange rates (which affect the prices to be paid by U.S. customers for foreign imports transported by the foreign competitors).

Chapter 16

(a) The forecasted cash balance of the U.S. parent will be reduced because the cost of imports are based on Mexican prices, which are to be revised upward.

(b) The forecasted cash balance of the U.S. parent will be increased because the foreign earnings remitted and British pound payments for exports will convert to a higher number of dollars (due to a downward revision of the dollar's strength).

(c) The forecasted cash balance of the U.S. parent will be reduced because there will be less foreign earnings after taxes, so less foreign earnings will be remitted to the U.S. parent.

Chapter 17

(a) Investment in marks:
$$r = (1 + .10) \times [1 + (-.01)] - 1$$
$$= 8.9\%$$
Investment in pesos:
$$r = (1 + .32) \times [1 + (-.20)] - 1$$
$$= 5.6\%$$

(b) Jordan should invest its funds in the U.S. because the yield from investing in dollars is highest and there is no exchange rate risk.

(c) Jordan may be able to use the peso proceeds from its Mexican investment to be received in one year to pay for imports from Mexico that are occurring at that time. In this way, there is no exposure to exchange rate risk when investing in pesos.

Chapter 18

(a) A somewhat lenient policy may be considered, given that the hospitals are backed by the British government. Jordan could request payment within 20 days or so after the goods are received. It could consider using letters of credit but may feel that such a guarantee is not worth the cost, because the risk of default on payment is low.

(b) A strict credit policy may be more appropriate for firms which Jordan deals with on an infrequent basis. Letters of credit or factoring should be considered.

Chapter 19

(a) The demand for supplies should rise as the British firms attempt to purchase the supplies before the dollar strengthens.

(b) In the scenario provided, the British customers could shift their demand to British or French firms. The decision to shift to French firms may depend on the exchange rate between the pound and the French franc.

(c) The Canadian subsidiary has a higher cost of carrying its inventory because its interest rates are typically higher. (The interest rate is the key factor that causes carrying costs to vary among countries.)

Chapter 20

(a) $\quad r_t = (1 + .08) \times [1 + (-.02)] -1$
$\quad\quad = 5.84\%$

(b) Some firms may be willing to borrow with yen because of the lower expected cost as compared to borrowing dollars at 10 percent. However, there is the risk that the yen may appreciate over time, which could cause its financing rate to exceed the interest rate when borrowing dollars.

(c) Jordan could instruct its Japanese subsidiary to use part of its earnings to repay the yen loan given to the parent in one year.

Chapter 21

(a) The cash inflows will be influenced by demand for the products, which will be affected by: (1) the economic conditions in East European countries (the higher the income levels, the higher the demand), (2) the exchange rate between the mark and the East European currencies (a weaker mark would increase demand), and (3) the intensity of competition.

The cash outflows will be influenced by production costs at the German subsidiary, the costs of promoting the products in East Europe, transportation costs, and taxes.

(b) There is more uncertainty about the number of units sold, because the demand would be very uncertain. Price per unit is heavily influenced by production costs per unit, which can be accurately estimated.

Chapter 22

(a) The appreciation of the franc causes a higher level of dollar cash flows to be received by the U.S. parent, and therefore makes the project more feasible than before.

(b) The higher long-term risk-free interest rate of the U.S. will cause the U.S. parent to use a higher required rate of return on the project, which will make the project less feasible than before.

Chapter 23

(a) The subsidiary in Japan would normally have a lower cost of capital, because its risk-free interest rate is usually lower than the rate in Germany. Therefore, the cost of debt would be lower, and the subsidiary's cost of capital is dictated by the cost of debt, since most of their funds were assumed to be obtained by borrowing.

(b) The cost of equity is composed of the risk-free rate and an equity risk premium. The risk-free rate is not affected by the location of the project, since the funding comes from U.S. shareholders. However, the equity risk premium would likely be higher for the project in Mexico because the success of the project would be influenced by the local economy, which is more volatile than the U.S. economy. Thus, the earnings from the Mexican project are possibly more uncertain. In addition, when the peso earnings are remitted there may be much uncertainty about the exchange rate that will exist at that time. Since the dollar cash flows to be received by the U.S. parent (which essentially belong to the shareholders) from the Colorado subsidiary are more certain than those from the Mexican subsidiary, the equity risk premium would be higher for the Mexican subsidiary.

Chapter 24

(a) Based on prevailing interest rates, the Canadian subsidiary should use an equity-intensive capital structure, while the Japanese subsidiary should use a debt-intensive capital structure. The German subsidiary falls somewhere in between.

(b) Based on exchange rate expectations, the Japanese subsidiary should use a debt-intensive capital structure, which reduces the amount of remitted funds to the parent over time, and therefore reduces exposure to exchange rate risk. The German subsidiary should use an equity-intensive capital structure. The Canadian subsidiary falls somewhere in between.

(c) Based on the small amount of information, the Canadian and German subsidiaries should use an equity-intensive capital structure, while the Japanese subsidiary should use a debt-intensive capital structure.

Chapter 25

(a) The bond offering would be more appropriate because the currency received matches the currency needed to support operations. If stock denominated in dollars was offered, the proceeds would have to be converted to the foreign subsidiary's respective currency. This results in greater exposure to exchange rate risk, because more funds would be remitted to the parent over time (since the subsidiary would not have the interest payments on debt if the bond offering does not occur). Given that the dollar is expected to strengthen, the remitted funds would convert to less dollars.

(b) The foreign subsidiaries would generate higher cash flows after expenses if Jordan Co. issued stock, because they would not incur interest payments on the debt.

Chapter 26

(a) Jordan's return on investment will be favorably affected if the British pound appreciates, because earnings remitted by the British subsidiary will be increased upon conversion of a stronger pound.

(b) Jordan should not defer the purchase, because the cost of obtaining pounds is expected to increase in the future. Jordan should consider making the purchase immediately.

Chapter 27

(a) Economic and industry conditions vary among countries, which can affect demand for the product, and costs of producing the product.

(b) The executive did not recognize that when the Canadian and German subsidiaries are performing similar to the U.S. parent, Jordan's overall performance is very sensitive to the U.S. conditions. The Japanese subsidiary is the only subsidiary whose performance was somewhat independent of the other subsidiaries.

Chapter 28

(a) Jordan could hedge by purchasing put options on yen.

(b) Advantage of put option over forward sale: Jordan can allow the put option to expire if the yen appreciates against the dollar, whereas it would be obligated by a forward contract to sell the yen at the rate specified in the forward contract.

(c) Disadvantage of put option relative to forward sale: A premium must be paid to purchase put options. If the yen depreciated as expected, it would have been cheaper to use forward contracts.

Chapter 29

(a) Canadian demand will decrease if the Canadian dollar weakens over time. British demand will decrease because the British customers will have to pay more as the pound weakens over time.

(b) No. It was implied earlier that Spark's profit margin is already low. If it cuts the price, it will reduce the profit margin further.

(c) No. Even though the profit margin at the production plant is insensitive to exchange rates, the cash flows generated from exports by the Detroit subsidiary are affected by the Canadian dollar's exchange rates. In addition, the costs of the shirts to the British subsidiary are affected by the pound's exchange rate. As cash flows of its subsidiaries are affected, the perceived value of Spark Co. should be affected as well.

(d) First, consider that the Detroit subsidiary will be adversely affected as the Canadian dollar weakens, because the Canadian customers will have to pay more for the Detroit subsidiary's exports. The Detroit subsidiary does not have much flexibility to lower its price to counter the exchange rate effect, as its profit margin is already low.

Second, consider that the British subsidiary's costs of purchasing the shirts from the U.S. production plant will rise as the pound weakens. If the British subsidiary tries to pass the higher costs on to customers by charging a higher price, the demand for its shirts will decline (because local competitors were not affected by the exchange rates, and will not have to adjust their prices for this reason).

Spark could consider strategies to counter the potential loss resulting from the decline in exchange rates. First, it could revise its marketing to focus more on the U.S. and less on the foreign countries. That is, it could attempt to increase its business in the U.S. to make up for a possible loss in its export business. In this way, it may be able to at least maintain its total sales volume.

It is probably not wise to increase marketing efforts in Canada and England because there are substitute products available. The price was the key to the success; extra marketing will probably not create product differentiation.

(e) Not necessarily! Even if Spark Co. diversifies across England, all sales in England will be exposed to movements in the value of the pound. The firm's performance may be less sensitive to U.S. conditions, but would be more sensitive to conditions and exchange rates in England. Thus, the profitability may be just as volatile as before.

(f) Spark Co. will be adversely affected by the future depreciation of the pound, because the proceeds received by the British subsidiary will convert to fewer dollars over time. Thus, it may wish to hedge.

Spark Co. would be better off selling pounds forward, based on its expectations. Both hedging techniques lock in future exchange rate of $1.70. However, if the pound is expected to depreciate by at least 3 percent, the forward rate is a cheaper hedge. Spark would have to pay a $.03 premium per unit on the put option. While the put option allows Spark Co. the flexibility to let the option expire, this flexibility is only beneficial if the pound does not depreciate. Since Spark is confident that the pound will depreciate, it should sell pounds forward with a forward contract instead of buying a put option. (The key is to stress the risk–return tradeoff involved here.)

(g) The U.S. investment is more feasible. Even though the British Treasury bills have a slightly higher yield, the effective yield of the British investment to a U.S. investor will be reduced by depreciation in the pound. If the pound depreciated by 3 percent over the year, the effective (exchange rate–adjusted) yield would be:

$$(1 + .09) \times [1 + (-.03)] - 1$$
$$= 5.73\%$$

If the depreciation is more than 3 percent, the effective yield would be even less.

(h) Financing with pounds appears to be less costly because the effective financing rate would be lower if Spark's forecast for the pound is correct. If the pound depreciates by 3 percent, the effective financing rate would be:

$$(1 + .10) \times [1 + (-.03)] -1 = 6.7\%$$

If the pound depreciates by more than 3 percent, this effective financing rate would be even lower.

If Spark Co. is quite confident that the pound will depreciate by at least 3 percent, it should consider financing with pounds. However, many firms would prefer the use of dollars, rather than be subject to the risk that the pound appreciates. Given the volatility of exchange rates, firms can not be too sure about the future value of a currency.

(i) First, any shift in production to England will reduce production in the U.S., which causes lower utilization of the plant in the U.S.

Regarding exchange rate risk, when Spark Co. builds a plant in England using U.S. dollars, it would convert the dollars to pounds today to pay for the construction. Over time, pound profits would be converted to dollars as they are remitted to the U.S. If the pound weakens over time as expected, the remitted earnings would be adversely affected. In essence, this strategy is still exposed to exchange rate risk, since Spark converted dollars to pounds at the initial investment stage, and periodically converts pounds back to dollars in subsequent years. Spark may be able to hedge this exposure, but there are easier ways to attempt a hedge than to build a foreign plant.

(j) If the pound depreciates over time, the profits of the British plant would be translated at a lower exchange rate, which would reduce the consolidated earnings of Spark Co.

(k) Spark could hedge the translation effects by selling pounds forward. If the pound depreciated, the forward contract position would generate a gain, which could offset the translation loss.

Since its consolidated earnings will be reduced by a weakening of the pound, Spark may consider hedging the translation effects. However, if the pound appreciates over time, there will be a translation gain, and the forward contract position will result in a loss.

Answers to End-of-Chapter Discussion Questions   219

Some firms are not comfortable with hedging translation effects, because if the foreign currency appreciates, a "paper" gain is offset by a "cash" loss. There is no perfect solution to this question, but the question should lead to an interesting classroom discussion.

(l) The financing costs of maintaining inventory can vary across countries because interest rates vary across countries. If the interest rates are higher in the United Kingdom, the cost of maintaining inventory there should be higher.